Christian pilgrimage in the Middle Ages was not just an act of piety. It was deeply bound up with pre-Reformation man's main concern —the salvation of his soul. For this reason the pilgrimage to Compostela has been described as a key to the literary, artistic and cultural understanding of the Middle Ages. Everyone went on pilgrimage, from kings and bishops to monks and millers, and for over a thousand years an endless succession of priests, visionaries and cynics denounced the practice.

The introduction to this book examines pilgrimages in the context of medieval Christianity, to find out why people went on them, who went on them, and where they went, from the fourth century to about 1500. A section is then devoted to miracles, relics and indulgences. In the body of the book the pilgrimage itself is recreated, drawing on diaries, chronicles, letters, state papers, references in contemporary literature and surviving archives from hospices and religious foundations, some available for the first time in English. Individual subsections are devoted to preparations for the voyage, the routes followed and hazards encountered on the journey, practical matters of organisation, accommodation, arrival at the shrine and, finally, departure. Four later sections then deal with each of the major places of pilgrimage in the Middle Ages.

A valuable addition to the WAYLAND DOCUMENTARY HISTORY SERIES, this book is illustrated with many woodcuts, manuscript illuminations and other pictures drawn from contemporary sources.

Frontispiece A Veronese pilgrim with staff and beads

Medieval Pilgrims

by Alan Kendall

WAYLAND PUBLISHERS LONDON

SBN (hardback edition): 85340 006 7
SBN (limp edition): 85340 208 6
Second impression 1972
Copyright © 1970 by Wayland (Publishers) Ltd
101 Grays Inn Road, London WC1
Photoset and printed by BAS Printers Limited, Wallop, Hampshire

Contents

List of Illustrations

Introduction

'THE DESIRE to be a pilgrim,' says Sir Steven Runciman, 'is deeply rooted in human nature. To stand where those that we reverence once stood, to see the very sites where they were born and toiled and died, gives us a feeling of mystical contact with them and is a practical expression of our homage. And if the great men of the world have their shrines to which their admirers come from afar, still more do men flock eagerly to those places where, they believe, the Divine has sanctified the earth (1).'

As early as the beginning of the third century, according to Eusebius of Caesarea (*c*.260–*c*.340), a bishop from Cappadocia made a pilgrimage to Rome, and St Jerome (*c*.342–420) wrote of similar early visits to the Holy Land. Constantine's work of pacification in the early fourth century had made possible the rebuilding of Jerusalem and the visit there of his mother, St Helena, in 326. It was there that this—according to Runciman—'most exalted and most successful of the world's great archaeologists' discovered the Cross on which our Lord was crucified. Constantine celebrated the event by building the Church of the Holy Sepulchre in Jerusalem and, ever since, the pilgrimage there, and to the Holy Land in general, has been the most highly prized by devout Christians.

Inspired by the discovery, or 'Invention', of the Cross of our Lord by St Helena, a stream of pilgrims began to flow towards the Holy Land. St Jerome actually settled there, and was followed by the fashionable ladies who had admired him in Italy. Even so, he stressed that the court of Heaven could be reached as well from Britain as Jerusalem: *et de Hierusolymis et de Britannia aequaliter patet aula coelestis*. The fathers of the Church knew only too well

The first pilgrims

11

Facing page Veneration of a saintly shrine

the dangers involved in mass pilgrimage, and later events proved them right. Throughout the period there was repeated anti-pilgrimage invective. St Boniface (680–754) complained that, in spite of the decrees of synods and kings, most women making pilgrimages to Rome lost their virtue. An eighth-century Irish poem runs: 'To go Rome means great labour and little profit; the king you seek can only be found there if you bring him within yourself (2).'

St Bernard of Clairvaux (1090–1153)—although he himself was to call for the Second Crusade—put it even more simply: 'Your cell is Jerusalem.' He also deplored their pride in relics and the bad faith of the Cluniac monks. The author of the *Imitation of Christ*, traditionally St Thomas à Kempis (*c.*1380–1471), says: 'Those who wander much are but little hallowed,' and the fifteenth-century English Dominican, John Bromyard: 'There are some who keep their pilgrimages and festivals not for God but for the devil. They who sin more freely when away from home or who go on pilgrimage to succeed in inordinate and foolish love—those who spend their time on the road in evil and uncharitable conversation may indeed say *peregrinamur a domino*—they make their pilgrimage away from God and to the Devil (3).'

Sir Thomas More

Sir Thomas More made a defence of pilgrimages in 1529, but Erasmus (*c.*1466–1536), in his *Coloquies*, disagreed. He felt that the home was neglected during pilgrimage; he deplored the superstition shown by the faithful as to relics and the legends surrounding them —also, presumably, in the cult of the saints generally. He denied that pilgrimages were necessary to salvation, and severely criticised

Facing page St Bernard of Clairvaux reading to fellow monks from the Bible

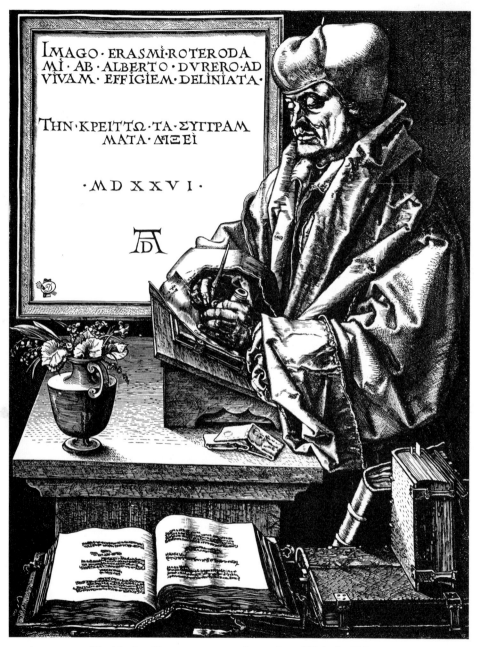

Desiderius Erasmus, a woodcut after Albrecht Dürer

the immorality of the pilgrims. However, Erasmus showed more humane enlightenment: 'I must own that these things had better be left undone, but when a thing cannot be at once corrected, I am wont to gather from it whatever good I can.'

By now we have come a long way from the medieval world. Yet *Erasmus* Erasmus still felt that pilgrimages were justified if they were begun freely and with piety: 'If any shall do it of their own free choice from a great affection to piety, I think they deserve to be left to their own freedom.' If nothing else, this shows how popular pilgrimages were, even at this late stage. Why was this?

Adam and Eve with the serpent and tree of knowledge

According to Christian belief, man is a fallen, sinful creature in *Polycarp* need of salvation. The finest pilgrimage, therefore, is that made freely by man for the salvation of his soul. But long before the time of St Augustine (354–430) it was felt that full remission of sins could be obtained by going to the tomb of a martyr and meditating there. When Polycarp, the first Christian martyr, died in Smyrna in

15

AD 155, his fellow Christians wrote: 'We recovered his bones, rarer than gold and more precious than costly jewels. We laid them in a fitting place. May the Lord grant us to assemble there, whenever we are able, in joy and gladness, to celebrate the anniversary of his martyrdom.'

The passion and triumph of a martyr was a renewal of the passion and triumph of Christ. By meeting to celebrate the Eucharist on the anniversary of his death, the faithful joined with the martyr in transcending historical time and praying for the Day of the Lord, which the martyr had already proclaimed by his sacrifice and victory. It soon became usual to celebrate Mass over his remains. As well as explaining the importance of martyrs, this shows how their relics came to play such a vital part in popular piety, as we shall see later (pp. 25–9). *Martyrs' shrines*

Apart from the Holy Land, where Christ had lived and died, the most popular places of pilgrimage were the tombs of SS Peter and Paul in Rome and St James at Compostela in Spain (where his remains were found in 830). Soon, however, non-martyrs' tombs were venerated, such as those of St Martin of Tours (d.397) and St Nicholas of Myra (now known as Santa Claus), whose body was taken to Bari in Italy in the eleventh century. Penitents, such as Mary Magdalene, were also included. The great church at Vézelay in France, dedicated to her memory, was one of the setting-off places for pilgrimages to Compostela. *Popular centres*

Many pilgrims hoped for nothing more from their travels than the joy of reaching the holy place (*ad limina*, from Lat. *limen*, threshold) and there steeping themselves in the martyr or saint's *virtus* and obtaining full forgiveness of their sins. But saints could also be asked to help cure the various ills of soul and body, and here we see an early and understandable extension of the purpose of pilgrimage. By such an act a believer could seek aid or, if he had already received it, give thanks. *Pilgrims' motives*

These acts of invocation and thanksgiving are inextricably entwined. But we can see now the dangers that the early fathers had foreseen in this extension of pilgrimage. What began as a search for better means of salvation and the life hereafter was in danger of being swamped by the hope of benefits to be obtained in the here and now. Of course, much of Christ's ministry had been devoted

17

Facing page Monks celebrating a requiem Mass, from an illuminated psalter

to healing the sick, and so it was natural that, in sickness and disease, the pilgrims should turn to the saints for help. But soon many other favours were solicited—the freeing of a prisoner, victory in time of war, or success in other activities. Some Christians, such as the fifteenth-century Dominican friar Brother Felix Fabri, had a consuming desire, once they had actually been there, to return to the Holy Land simply because of the joy they had experienced there. But at the other end of the scale there were people whose curiosity outran their piety. Sir John Mandeville supposedly set out for the Holy Land in 1322, unashamedly hunting new and marvellous experiences. He wanted to become an expert and

A pilgrim from Erasmus's *Praise of Folly*

seasoned traveller, though at the same time he probably also really hoped for personal sanctification.

Pilgrimage as
penance
In all fairness to the travellers, however, the decision to travel abroad in the Middle Ages was not one to be taken lightly, as we shall see. The status accorded pilgrims shows that to take up the staff amounted to answering a vocation. In fact pilgrimage was often imposed as a penance. An English canon law, dating from the reign of King Edgar (959–75) states: 'It is a deep penitence that a layman lay aside his weapons and travel far barefoot and nowhere pass a second night and fast and watch much and pray fervently, by day and by night and willingly undergo fatigue and be so squalid

18

that iron come not on hair or on nail (4).' This custom had begun under Popes Nicholas I (858–67) and Stephen V (885–91), when pilgrimages took the place of penances. It was soon extended to civil and criminal law penalties, as well.

Excommunication gave way to banishment or exile as punishment for the crimes of heresy, murder, arson, or the breaking of God's peace. The condemned could dress as a pilgrim, and had a safe conduct to a particular shrine. Later, with the development of Canon Law, the usual penalty for striking a cleric was a pilgrimage to Rome, since the pope was the only person able to absolve this crime. However, with the rise of the universities in the twelfth and

Two pilgrims of the early Reformation period

thirteenth centuries, so many students took advantage of this rule that it was abolished. We find a decree of the Parliament of Champagne dated 9 January 1367 under which Margaret, wife of Vicomte Ponsard Larrabis, petitions that a certain Stephen (who had called her names and beaten her) should atone by making a pilgrimage first to St Thomas of Canterbury and then to St James of Galicia [Compostela]; and that he should live in each place a year at his own expense, and bring back letters showing that he has done so. A wise precaution.

At this time one of the earls of Arundel obtained absolution for poaching on the bishop's land at Hoghton Chace, on condition that

19

he made a pilgrimage to the shrine of St Richard of Chichester. The distance involved was slight. More important was his public submission, as a noble, to the Church. On the Continent, in the Low Countries, lay courts could sentence offenders to pilgrimage long after the Church had stopped the practice of public penance.

'Deputy pilgrims'   Sometimes pilgrimages were carried out by deputy. We read in the *Register of Henry Chichele*, an Archbishop of Canterbury (?1362–1443), that under the terms of his will, 'a good and suitable person, a chaplain' is to be chosen to carry out a pilgrimage for him. John Paston wrote to his mother Margaret, then in London, on 14 September 1465: 'I pray you visit the rood of Northdoor [of St Paul's Cathedral] and St Saviour, at Bermondsey [Southwark], among while you abide in London, and let my sister Margery go with you to pray to them that she may have a good husband ere she come home again (5).'

Anyone at all might go on a pilgrimage, though the doings of the rich and famous are naturally better documented for the early period than those of ordinary folk. So many are said to have followed St Columbanus from Ireland after 590 that Gozbert, in his life of St Gall, remarked: 'Of late so many Scots [Irish] are pilgrims that it would appear that the habit of travelling is part of their nature.' One often meets expressions such as *peregrinans pro Dei amore* or *pro nomine Christi* ('wandering for the love of God' or 'for the name of Christ') in the lives of the Irish saints, and St Molua, who died about 608, set out on pilgrimage saying 'Unless I see Rome, I will die soon.'

Not all pilgrims were so dramatically drawn to their goals, however, though many returned to the places where they had found comfort. Charlemagne went to Rome at least four times. Duke William V of Aquitaine (*c*.1000) went each year either to Rome or Compostela. One of the first acts of Richard Lionheart (1157–99) after his release from captivity in Germany after the Third Crusade, was to visit the

Emperor Charlemagne holding an orb in one hand and a sword in the other

Funeral procession of Edward the Confessor from an
early manuscript drawing

tomb of Edward the Confessor in Westminster Abbey.

Louis IX (St Louis, 1214–70) went barefoot five leagues to Chartres. Charles VII of France (1403–61) went five times to Le Puy, where there was a shrine to the Virgin Mary, and his son Louis XI (1423–83) went to Notre Dame de Béhuard in Anjou fifteen times. Pope Pius II (Enea Silvio Piccolomini, 1405–64) walked barefoot through the snow to Our Lady of Whitekirk in East Lothian, Scotland. He remembered it all his life because it led to a severe attack of gout.

Example of kings and popes

When kings and popes set such an example, lesser mortals wanted to do the same. The senior member of feudal society on Chaucer's pilgrimage to Canterbury was the Knight; this is understandable for a group that met almost by chance. The canons of Hereford Cathedral laid down that none of them was to make more than one pilgrimage beyond the seas in his own lifetime. Each year three weeks were allowed for visits to shrines within the kingdom. To go abroad to the tomb of St Denis near Paris, seven weeks of absence was permitted. Eight weeks were allowed for a visit to the body of St Edmund of Canterbury at Pontigny in France, sixteen weeks to Rome, or to Santiago de Compostela, and a year to Jerusalem.

Dante, in *La Vita Nuova*, defined the word 'pilgrim': '. . . "pilgrim" may be understood in two senses, one general, and

Chaucer's knight from a manuscript
edition of *The Canterbury Tales*

21

Dante

one special. General, so far as any man may be called a pilgrim who leaveth the place of his birth; whereas, more narrowly speaking, he only is a pilgrim who goeth towards or forwards the House of St James. For there are three separate denominations proper unto those who undertake journeys to the glory of God. They are called Palmers who go beyond the seas eastward [to the Holy Land], whence often they bring palm-branches. And Pilgrims, as I have said, are they who journey unto the holy House of Galicia; seeing that no other apostle was buried so far from his birth-place as was blessed St James; and there is a third sort who are called Romers; in that they go whither those whom I have called pilgrims went: which is to say, unto Rome (6).'

Modern survivals

Whatever one may regret in the passing of medieval Christianity, one must surely be grateful for the resulting benefits. The material glory of many of the shrines has long since disappeared, particularly in countries Protestant today, and even in Roman Catholic countries many of the reliquaries and pious devotional objects are shut away in vestry cupboards. And yet Lourdes survives, with its special

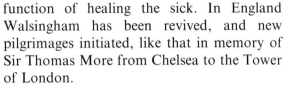

function of healing the sick. In England Walsingham has been revived, and new pilgrimages initiated, like that in memory of Sir Thomas More from Chelsea to the Tower of London.

Yet Christians do think of life as a pilgrimage, a mere prelude to the hereafter. As the author of the *Epistle to the Hebrews* put it: 'For here we have no continuing city, but we seek one to come.' The final goal of the soul is not the earthly but the heavenly Jerusalem. Even long after the end of the Middle Ages, Bunyan's *Pilgrim's Progress* made a great restatement of the idea of pilgrimage in Christian life. Then, the pilgrim had no automatic right to the merits of pilgrimage. He had to earn them. As the Old Testament prophets kept reminding the Jews, and the Church over the ages has reminded herself, no amount of good deeds can replace faith.

Bunyan's dream: the frontispiece to the 1680 edition of *Pilgrim's Progress. Facing page* A fearful medieval view of Hell

'I am going to my Father's; and though with great difficulty I have got hither, yet now I do not repent me of all the trouble I have been at to arrive where I am. My sword I give to him that shall succeed me in my pilgrimage, and my courage and skill to him that can get it. My marks and scars I carry with me, to be a witness for me that I have fought His battles, who now will be my rewarder.'

The shrine of Edward the Confessor

1 Relics, miracles and indulgences

WE HAVE seen how the Church from earliest times gave special *Relics* veneration to martyrs. In the Roman liturgy martyrs rank higher than any other saints. We have also seen that their mortal remains were highly regarded by the living, at first simply for their association with the martyr and for the sacrifice they represented. To this day, in the Roman Catholic Church, an altar cannot be properly consecrated unless it contains the relics of a martyr. But the process did not stop there. People began to talk of miraculous cures at the tomb; the relics themselves became more precious still.

Leave aside the case for and against miracles: the Church has *Miracles* always required that before declaring a person a saint, he or she must be beatified. For this two to four authenticated miracles should have been performed by the person in question. Yet the Church has never required belief in miracles as a matter of faith. Be that as it may, miracles have always enthralled the mind of man, and in an age of widespread faith such as the Middle Ages, every 'miracle' was acclaimed; and the relics of the saints who were not martyrs also came to inspire the faithful. In fact 'confessors'— those who had suffered but not died for the faith—were venerated quite early on. St Martin of Tours, who died towards the end of the fourth century, was one.

Once the idea of a pilgrimage to the tomb of a saint was accepted, *Apparitions* it soon extended to places where anything supernatural had been seen. These included Ambronay in Burgundy from the seventh century, and Einsiedeln in Switzerland from 954, where people claimed to have seen the Virgin Mary. Savona, near Genoa in Italy, actually dated from the time of Constantine. The pilgrimage to

25

A medieval reliquary in which saintly relics were kept

Monte Gargano in Apulia, Italy, began after an apparition of St Michael. What troubled the ecclesiastical authorities a great deal was that old pagan shrines were often simply adapted to Christian use. At Fourvière, near Lyons in France, a shrine to the Virgin Mary had once been dedicated to the god Mercury. Pagan statues sometimes became Christian: the gold bust of St Foy of Conques is almost certainly an example.

Medieval piety   The piety of the Middle Ages was irrepressible. Here is William de Grenefield, Archbishop of York, writing in 1313: 'We have learned that a statue of the Blessed Virgin newly installed in the parish church of Foston is stirring up many simple souls as if something divine were more apparent in this statue than in others (7).'

There was no end to the desire to hallow, venerate and sanctify.

People so prone to venerate holy places and the shrines of the saints soon venerated their remains or relics in the same way. As early as the fifth century Achilleus, Bishop of Spoleto, warned the

26

Facing page Gabriel tells of the birth of Christ, as pictured by a medieval illuminator

PERA

CONSTAN=
NOPOLIS

porta del meso

Ses demet

Ses geor
gius

palaci imperagus

Ses Johes dipp

chiramos

portus olim
palacii im
peratoris

porta

Calchi

Ses Johes d'
andr

blangn

portus sed destruct
precepto teucrorum

countless pilgrims who passed through his city on the Via Flaminia, bound for Rome, against superstition about relics. At the end of the next century, Queen Theodolinda of the Lombards asked Pope Gregory I for the head of a saint to grace the new basilica she had built at Monza. Gregory replied that he dare not do this. Instead, he sent ampules filled with oil that had been burning in the lamps at shrines of some sixty-five martyrs. Each ampule was identified as to its source.

The demand for relics grew, and where it was not possible to find new ones or divide the old ones, pilgrims found substitutes. Fragments of wood, stone—even dust—were reverently collected because they came from a particular shrine. Scraps of cloth were dipped in oil in the lamps in front of the shrines, and then carried away. Knights would have relics fitted into the pommels of their swords. Whilst the demand existed, the supply was kept up. The sack of Constantinople in 1204 put a whole new wave of relics onto the market, including the Crown of Thorns. For this St Louis built the Sainte Chapelle in Paris, little short of a reliquary in glass and stone. *Collecting relics*

Until we appreciate the medieval state of mind, the whole idea of the pre-Reformation pilgrimage will be lost on us. Emile Mâle has said that the pilgrimage to Compostela is a key to the literary, artistic and cultural understanding of the Middle Ages; the rest of this book will try to show just how far medieval life was permeated with the idea of pilgrimage.

Finally, a word about indulgences. The *New Catholic Encyclopedia* states: '[Indulgences are] authoritative grants from the Church's treasury for the remission or payment in whole (plenary indulgences) or in part (partial indulgences), valid before God, of the debt of temporal punishment after the guilt of sin has been forgiven. An indulgence grant in the strict sense of the term is not met with until the early decades of the eleventh century … and yet the principle underlying the indulgence grant is as old as the Church herself.' Catholics believe we all have a debt to pay, either here on earth or afterwards in purgatory, even though we might go through the process of penitence and receive absolution, and so be reconciled to God. Although the actual text of his speech has not survived, when Urban II preached the First Crusade at the Council of *Indulgences*

Facing page Constantinople in the Middle Ages, when all the old Christian churches had been turned into mosques

Clermont in 1095 he is reported as saying: 'Whoever from devotion alone, and not for the purpose of gaining honours and wealth, shall set out for the liberation of the Church of God at Jerusalem, that journey will be reckoned in place of all penance (8).' Intending Crusaders had, of course, to make their confession first, but this was a prime example of a plenary indulgence.

Chaucer's Pardoner   The later Middle Ages saw many abuses creep into the use of the indulgence, in particular the 'pardoners' who went about selling indulgences, like Chaucer's Pardoner:

> '... when that he found
> A poor parson dwelling upon land,
> Upon a day he got him more money
> Than that the parson got in two months;
> And thus, with feigned flattery and japes,
> He made the parson and the people his apes.
>
>   *   *   *
>
> Well could he read a lesson or a story,
> But best of all he sang an offertory;
> For well he knew that when the song was sung,
> He must preach and well smooth his tongue
> To win silver, as full well he could (9).'

When Chaucer describes the Pardoner in the Prologue he is fairly kind to him, but when he lets the Pardoner speak for himself in the prologue to his tale, the cynicism put into his mouth is devastating. To begin with, and with bitter irony, the theme of his sermon, he tells us, is always *Radix malorum est cupiditas*—'love of money is the root of all evil'. He goes on:

> 'And whoso findeth him[self] out of such blame,
> He will come up and offer in God's name,
> And I absolve him by the authority
> Which by that bull granted was to me.
> By this trick I have won, year by year,
> An hundred marks since I was pardoner.
>
>   *   *   *
>
> Of avarice and of such cursedness
> Is all my preaching, for to make them free
> To give their pence, and namely unto me.

Left A medieval portrait of Chaucer in an early edition of the
Canterbury Tales and *right*, from the same edition, a picture
of Chaucer's Pardoner

> For my intent is only to win,
> And nothing for correction of sin.
> I care never, when that they have been buried,
> Though that their souls go a-blackberrying.'

Possibly Chaucer overdoes it in the end. It is hard to believe that
anyone could be like this. But the material undoubtedly existed.
Over a hundred years later the preacher and indulgence-seller
Johann Tetzel and his travelling circus in Germany so incensed
Luther that he was driven to issue his Ninety-Five Theses. The
profits that eventually reached Rome from Tetzel were to pay for
rebuilding St Peter's.

Perhaps we should let William Langland have the last word. He
can always be relied upon in *Piers Plowman* to give adverse comment
when needed in religious matters. Yet his earnestness and directness
are probably more telling than Chaucer's rather cavalier art:

Piers Plowman

'You who purchase your pardons and papal charters:
At the dread doom, when the dead shall rise
And all come before Christ, and give full accounting,
When the doom will decide what day by day you practised,
How you led your life and were lawful before him
Though you have pocketfuls of pardons there or provincial letters,
Though you be found in the fraternity of all the four orders,
Though you have double indulgences,—unless Do Well help you
I set not your patents and your pardons at the worth of a peascod! (10).'

Facing page The Martyrdom of St Peter by Berruguete

Flagellants of the fifteenth century. Flagellation was a form of spiritual purification to which pilgrims, penitents and others submitted

2 Preparations

BEFORE setting out, a pilgrim would put his affairs in order. This *Leaving home* often meant making his will, and paying back any money acquired dishonestly. He had to provide for his family during his absence and give alms, whilst leaving himself enough money for his journey. When Brother Fabri went on his second journey to the Holy Land he went as chaplain to a group of German aristocrats. Before leaving for Venice they went to Innsbruck, to entrust 'their wives, children, lands, villages, towns and castles, counties and lordships (11), to the care of the Duke of Austria. He in turn gave them 'letters commendatory' to the Doge and Senate of Venice.

To receive full benefit of the privileges to which a *bona fide* pilgrim *Permission* was entitled, and pilgrims were protected by several decrees *to go* passed by church councils and were in a way assimilated to the clergy; the pilgrim had to have the written permission of his bishop or, if he were a monk, his abbot. In fact by the twelfth and thirteenth centuries it was only the production of these special letters (*testimoniales*) that saved his being taken for an adventurer or a profiteer. An ordinance of Richard II, dated 1388, shows that any pilgrim found without his *testimoniales* risked arrest.

The pilgrim had special clothing, of which several descriptions *Pilgrim dress* survive. Here is Brother Fabri, before his second journey: 'So I from this day forth let my beard grow, and adorned both my cap and my scapular with red crosses, which crosses were sewn on to my clothes for me by virgins, dedicated to God, spouses of Him crucified; and I assumed all the other outward signs of that holy pilgrimage, as I had a right to do. There are five outward badges of a pilgrim, to wit, a red cross on a long grey gown, with the monk's

35

cowl sewn to the tunic—unless the pilgrim belong to some order which does not permit him to wear a grey gown. The second is a black or grey hat, also marked in front with a red cross. The third is a long beard growing from a face which is serious and pale ... The fourth is the scrip upon his shoulders, containing his slender provisions, with a bottle—sufficient, not for luxury, but barely for the necessaries of life. The fifth, which he assumes only in the Holy Land, is an ass, with a Saracen driver, instead of his staff.'

Another description is given in *Piers Plowman*:

'It was late and long when they lighted on a traveller
Apparelled like a pilgrim in pagan clothing.
He bore a staff bound with a broad fillet,
That like a winding weed wound about it.
At his belt he bore a bowl and wallet.
An hundred ampules hung at his hatband,
Signs from Sinai and shells from Galice [Compostela],
Many a cross on his cloak, and keys from Rome,
And the vernicle in front, that friends might find it,
And see by his signs what shrines he had been to.'

Perhaps the classic portrait is that given by Sir Walter Raleigh (1552–1618) in *The Pilgrimage*:

'Give me my scallop-shell of quiet,
My staff of faith to walk upon,
My scrip of joy, immortal diet,
My bottle of salvation,
My gown of glory, hope's true gage;
And thus I'll take my pilgrimage.'

Before the pilgrim set out he received a special blessing. Brother Fabri mentions it quite briefly, as something quite natural and so hardly worth a detailed description: 'Now on the fourteenth day of April, early in the morning, after I had received the blessing which is given to those who travel, and after I had kissed and embraced my brethren, we mounted our horses ...'

Blessing for the journey
36

Here is an extract from the *Sarum Missal*:
'*Blessing of Scrip and Staff*: The scrip is sprinkled with holy water and put around the pilgrim's neck by the priest. "In the name of

our Lord Jesus Christ receive this scrip, the habit of thy pilgrimage that after due chastisement thou mayest be found worthy to reach in safety the Shrine of the Saints to which thou desirest to go: and after the accomplishment of thy journey thou mayest return to us in health." Next the staff is given to the pilgrim, and then if the pilgrim is bound for Jerusalem, the cross is blessed. The garment is sprinkled with holy water and given to him.'

Sprinkling with holy water

Naturally the news that a person was to go on a pilgrimage excited his friends. With a little exaggeration perhaps, Fabri wrote: '... in the year of our Lord 1480, on the ninth day of the month of April ... I ascended the pulpit, and preached to the people who were present in great numbers, both to hear the sermon and to obtain indulgences. When I had finished my sermon ... I told them all of the pilgrimage which I was on the point of beginning, bidding them, and beseeching them, to importune God with prayers for my safe return and at the present time to sing with me in gladness ... nor did they refrain from tears, and some broke out into sobs instead of into song. For many persons of both sexes were anxious and alarmed, fearing, even as I myself feared, that I should perish among such terrible dangers.' *Excitement*

He did not perish. In fact he was so impressed with the Holy Land that he wanted to go back as soon as possible. The way he set about his return trip was slightly devious: he first obtained permission from the pope and only later asked the abbot of his monastery. He also induced the nobles, whose chaplain he would *Fabri's second pilgrimage*

37

be, to speak on his behalf. In the circumstances the abbot could hardly stop him going. Fabri threw himself into the preparations for the sea voyage from Venice with all the confidence of a seasoned traveller. On the sixth day they went to the market and bought 'cushions, mattresses, pillows, sheets, coverlets, mats, jars, and so forth, for each berth. I bade them buy a mattress for me stuffed with cow's hair, and I had brought woollen blankets with me from Ulm.' Fabri thought that it was wrong that he should be more comfortable on board ship than in his cell.

Eleventh-century English sailing vessels and boats, from a manuscript drawing

Patron saints   One of the last acts before setting sail was to visit the Venice churches whose patron saints were appropriate for people going on pilgrimage: St Raphael, St Michael, St Christopher and St Martha: 'and begged her that she would take care to provide us with good and honourable inns, or at all events provide us with patience to bear the shortcomings of our inns during our long journey.' We shall see later what conditions were like in medieval inns, but Fabri's experience was not entirely happy.

Finally, Fabri's feelings when setting out on his first voyage must have been shared by almost every pilgrim at some time or other.

Their directness enables us to feel very vividly what it must have been like: 'After my father's departure, a great and almost irresistible temptation assailed me, for the delightful eagerness to see Jerusalem and the holy places, with which I had until that time been glowing, altogether died within me, and I felt a loathing for travel; and the pilgrimage, which had appeared so sweet and virtuous, now seemed wearisome, bitter, useless, empty, and sinful.'

An English pilgrim wearing the pilgrim's traditional hat, beads, and staff

3 Accepted routes

Setting out

THE ORGANISATION of pilgrim routes and the erection of hospices was undertaken very early on by popes and secular rulers alike. As early as the fourth century Pope Damasus (*c.*302–84) organised a system of signposting—in the form of verse inscriptions—in the catacombs at Rome that lasted until the eighth century. In the sixth century Pope Symmachus (d.514) was greatly concerned for pilgrim welfare. King (and later Saint) Stephen of Hungary (975–1038) is remembered by the chronicler because: '… he made the way very safe for all and thus allowed by his benevolence a countless multitude both of noble and common people to start for Jerusalem (12).'

Organisation of routes

But then, as now, people rarely went abroad without first trying to find out something about the place they hoped to visit, and the most suitable route there. Several guide books were available, the earliest known as *intineraria*; these were probably based on Roman military maps and tax archives. Already in the time of Pope Honorius I (625–38) *notitia ecclesiarum urbis Romae* told pilgrims how to get from the church of SS John and Paul on the Caelian Hill to St Peter's, making a huge circle round the city from the Via Flaminia on the North to the churches and cemeteries on the East and South, and then West.

Guide books

The writing of guide books became quite popular, and in 1154 Roger of Sicily had the *Book of Roger, or the Delight of whoso loves to make the Circuit of the World* compiled from the stories of pilgrims and merchants, who were questioned by a panel of Arab experts. As we know, much of the reason for Sir John Mandeville's travels was the desire to be looked up to as an experienced traveller.

Facing page The Pilgrim, from a fifteenth century German woodcut

Four scenes of a pilgrim on his travels, woodcuts from *The Book of Pilgrims* (1486)

Probably more than anything else, this attitude to pilgrimage denoted the passing of the Middle Ages and the advent of the Renaissance. In the mid-fifteenth century we read in the correspondence between John Paston and one John Davy about the estate of Sir John Fastolf, and his employment of one Bussard: '... the last time that he [Bussard] wrote to William Wusseter, it was before midsummer, and then he wrote a chronicle of Jerusalem, and the journeys that my master [Sir John Fastolf] did while he was in France (that God on his soul have mercy!); and he said that this drew more than twenty whazeries [quires?] of paper ...'

The Guide du Pèlerin

John Paston was trying to recover any documents relating to the estate, and legal quarrels dragged on for several years. We are not sure what became of this chronicle, but luckily we have a *Guide du Pèlerin* (Pilgrim's Guide), possibly written by a twelfth-century monk from Poitou called Aimery Picaud. Picaud loved his own Poitou: '... after Tours, you find Poitou, fertile, excellent, and full of all felicities. Poitevins are vigorous people and good fighters, skilled in the handling of bows, arrows and lances, brave in the thick of battle, fleet of foot, elegant in their dress, fair of face, full of spirit, very generous, free with hospitality.'

Journey through Bordelais

Heading south for Spain, one comes next to: '... Bordelais [i.e. the area around Bordeaux] where the wine is excellent, fish abundant, but the speech rough. The people of Saintonge [an area to the

north of Bordeaux] already have a common manner of speaking, but that of Bordelais is even more so. Then you must count on three tiring days to cross the Landes Bordelais. It is a desolate country, where all is lacking; there is neither bread, nor wine, nor meat, nor fish, nor water, nor springs; villages are rare on this sandy plain which nevertheless abounds in honey, millet, panic [another sort of millet] and pigs. If by chance you cross the Landes in summer, make sure you protect your face from the enormous flies that proliferate there, and which they call wasps or horse-flies ...' This sort of information would be invaluable for a pilgrim who did not know the country.

When it comes to the Gascons, Picaud cannot resist an invidious comparison: 'The Gascons are light in words, talkative, mockers, debauchees, drunkards, gourmands, badly dressed in rags and un-provided with money; nevertheless they are trained to fight and noted for their hospitality to the poor. Seated around the fire, they eat without a table and drink out of the same goblet. They eat a lot, drink at a gulp and are badly dressed [Picaud seems obsessed about this fact]; they are not ashamed to sleep together on a meagre bedding of rotten straw, the servants with master and mistress.'

Journey through Gascony

Picaud complains bitterly of the extortion of ferrymen and customs officials and reminds local authorities to see that pilgrims are not victimised. (Since this concerns Compostela more closely, this material appears under that section, pp. 103–7).

Coming to Navarre, Picaud does not seem to have very much to say in its favour either: '... the whole household, servant and master, maid and mistress, eat all alike, out of the same stewpot, the food that has been mixed together there, and that with their hands, without recourse to spoons, and they drink from the same goblet (13).'

Had Picaud been able to meet Chaucer's Prioress almost three centuries later, he might still have found her lacking in manners, though Chaucer is at pains to point out how genteel she was:

> 'At meat well taught was she withal;
> Nor wet her fingers in her sauce deep;
> She let no morsel from her lips fall,
> Well could she carry a morsel and well keep
> That no drop fell upon her breast.
> In courtesy was set much her lust.'

Chaucer's Prioress, from an early manuscript edition of *The Canterbury Tales*

> 'Her over [upper] lip wiped she so clean
> That in her cup there was no farthing [spot] seen
> Of grease, when she had drunk her draught.
> Full seemly after her meat she stretched.'

One wonders how she would have managed with Fabri and his companions.

In order to give some ideas as to time for these journeys, a few
statistics might be quoted at this point. In 1139 Reynold of Evesham
took 49 days from Canterbury to Rome. In 1157 messengers from
St Albans to Rome took a similar 49 days each way from Canterbury, spending 104 days on the round trip and allowing 6 days in
Rome. In 1204 Thomas de Marleberg took 40 days from Evesham
to Rome, which probably means 38 days from London. But in 1224
two king's envoys went from Wicklow in Ireland to Rome in 39
days, which would mean 35 or even less from London. For ordinary
people this seems to have been the optimum time. The murder of
Henry of Almaine in Viterbo on 13 March 1271 was announced to
his father at Isleworth in Middlesex on 24 April, six weeks later.
Of course, faster journeys were possible for official business. In
1188 two papal mandates travelled from Rome to Canterbury in
29 and 25 days respectively (14). The Lord of Caumont on the
Garonne in France left for Rome on 8 July 1417 and returned on 3
September of the same year. Two years later he left for the Holy
Land on 27 February 1419 and returned on 14 April 1420.

One of the most exotic itineraries was that of Nikulas of Mun-
kathverá, who journeyed from Iceland to Rome over the Great
St Bernard in the mid-twelfth century. For the English traveller of
later years, however, there was a very useful book printed in 1498,
the first printed guidebook in English, called *Informacon for
pylgrymes unto the holy londe*.

There is also a manuscript handbook in the British Museum
which gives more good advice to pilgrims: '*Item*, be well advised
at Bruges, in the fellowship of such as make your exchange [for
money for the journey], of the most sure ways from town to town:
of the which there have been often divers, and one better than other,
because of war and other misdoers for the time (15).'

An interesting piece of advice makes one wonder as to the com-
parative financial standing of German tourists and that of the
Englishmen for whom these notes were intended. Fabri never seems
to have had any trouble with money, even on his first trip, and
certainly not on the second. Can the Germans have been the
(proverbial) Americans of the Middle Ages? 'At Padua, Treviso,
and Verona is good abiding if a man will sojourn or abide till his
passage were ready [this means until his ship was ready to set sail

from Venice], as at the Friars or some other hired house, if it might be got: for at the hostelries it would be over heavy and costly, were it at Venice or elsewhere (16).'

Fabri objected to his inn, not because it was expensive but because he missed his cell. This was laudable, but reveals an entirely different scale of values.

The English manuscript ends: 'the further ye go, the more ye shall see and know.' Already medieval piety was giving way to Renaissance curiosity. When Piers Plowman railed against those who travel in pilgrimage and leave behind them pain and suffering, he was championing a cause already lost:

> ' "adress me not," said Reason, "to have ruth on any
> Till lords and ladies love truth wholly,
> And leave all licence, listening to it or speaking it;
> Till religious roamers recordare in their cloisters
> As Saint Benet bad them, and Bernard and Francis;
>
>   *   *   *
>
> Till Saint James is sought as I assign it—
> In prisons, and poor huts, where the poor are lying—
> Till no man go to Galis [Compostela] unless he go forever;
> Till no runner to Rome bears, for robbers on the highway,
> Silver over seas, with the sign of the kingdom,
> Graven or ungraven, gold or silver,
> Or forfeit his fee, if they find it at Dover,
> Except merchants and their men, or messengers with letters,
> Provisors or priests or penitent sinners.
>
>   *   *   *
>
> And you who seek Saint James and the saints in Rome,
> Seek Saint Truth, who may save all men; ..."
> —Thus said Reason.'

Facing page Merchant ships like these English ones of the fifteenth century were the normal form of sea travel for pilgrims going to the Holy Land or other centres

...chard sailed towardes the holy londe and ...ly Cite of Jherlm, Where our lord Jhu ...ffered his bitter passion, for the redempcion ...nde.

specyally to the Cryste wilfully of al man

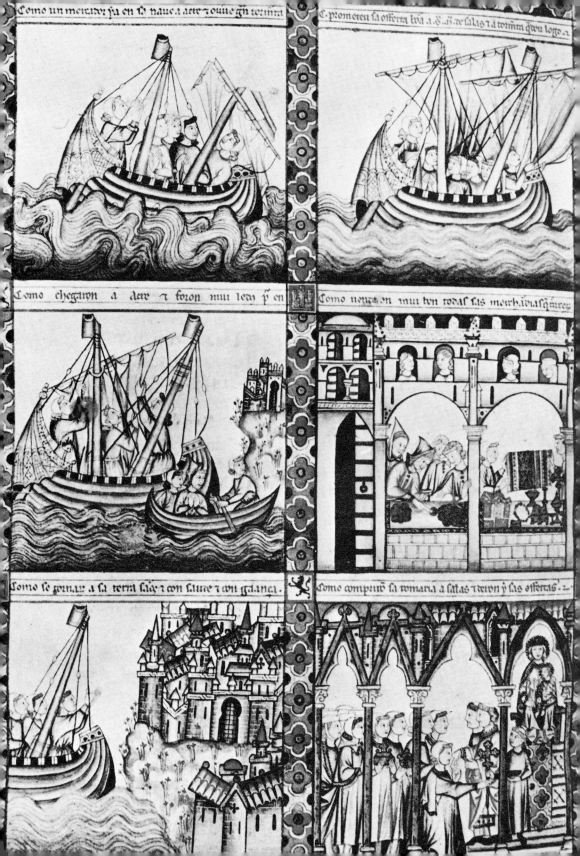

Como un mercador ya en ſa naue a aere e ouue gñ tormẽta

E prometeu ſa offerta bõa a ſ̄. ñ. de ſalas e a toꝛmẽ̃ta ꝑꝺeu logo ẽ.

Como chegaron a aere e foron muu ledos p̃ en

Como uẽꝺẽ̃ẽ muꝉ bẽ todas ſas mercaꝺuꝛias q̃ tꝛ̃.

Como ſe goꝛnaꝛ a ſa terꝛa ſãos e coꝭ ſaluo e con ganancia.

Como compꝛ̃u ſa romaria a ſcas Maria ẽ y ſas offertas.

4 Hazards of the journey

NOWADAYS man can hurtle through space and journey to the moon, *The weather*
but for earthbound mortals a good snowstorm will bring road
traffic to a standstill, and ground all aircraft. It is not surprising,
therefore, that the major hazard a pilgrim might face five hundred
years ago was the weather. Here is an account of the crossing of
Mont Cenis in January, 1077, by the German Emperor Henry IV:
'Then the men rose to overcome the danger by sheer exertion, now
crawling on hands and feet, now leaning on their guides, now stag-
gering and falling and rolling on the slippery slope, until at length
they reached the plain after severe fatigue. The queen and the
women in her company were installed in oxhides, and slid down by
their guides. Some of the horses were lowered by certain devices,
others were slid down with their legs bound; but many of them
were killed in their course, many were much weakened, only a few
came through whole and unharmed (17).' One questions the wisdom
of having set out in January.

Here, a few years later in 1188, is Brother John of Canterbury:
'Forgive my not writing. I have been on the Mons Jovis. [Great
St Bernard] ... I put my hand in my scrip to scratch out a word or
two to your sincerity: behold I found my ink-bottle filled with a
dry mass of ice. My fingers refused to write; my beard was stiff
with frost, and my breath congealed in a long icicle. I could not
write (18).'

For travellers at sea, a storm brought terror and panic (Fabri): *Perils of the*
'Meanwhile the pilgrims and those who were useless at this work *sea*
[of retrieving a loose sail] prayed to God and called upon the saints.
Some made their confessions as though already at the very point of

Facing page These six scenes from an illuminated manuscript
depict ships voyaging to the Holy Land. Notice the storm
(*top left*) and joyful arrival at the Holy Land (*bottom left*)

death; some made great vows that they would travel hence to Rome, to St James [of Compostela], or to the house of the Blessed Virgin [Loreto], if only they might escape from this death; for it is only when death is present before our eyes that we fear it.' The ship's best officer had previously been killed by a block falling from the masthead. Against similar minor and major disasters—such as the fire at Vézelay in 1120, in which 1,000 pilgrims died—there is no real protection even today.

If two countries were at war, a wise pilgrim kept away. In any case, unless he was sought as a hostage, his pilgrim status did count for something. Agnes Paston wrote in 1450 to her grandson John (one of them; there were two), who was then in London at the Inner Temple: 'Richard Lynsted came this day from Paston, and told me that on Saturday last past Dravale, half-brother to Waryn Harman, was taken with enemies, walking by the seaside, and have him forth with them; and they took two pilgrims, a man and a woman, and they robbed the woman, and let her go, and had the man to the sea, and when they knew he was a pilgrim, they gave him money, and set him again on the land.' The 'enemies', possibly the French, were the aggressors in this instance, but one must bear in mind that there were countless messengers and spies dashing around Europe, and it was easy enough for them to pose as pilgrims. *In time of war*

Others posed as Scots, as we see from this delightful story of Samson, later Abbot of Bury, who took an appeal to Rome in 1161 when Barbarossa was supporting an anti-pope (Victor IV) against Alexander III: 'I crossed Italy in that storm in which all clerics who bore Alexander's letters were seized: some were imprisoned, some hanged, some had their lips and noses cut off and were sent on thus to the pope to his disgrace and shame. For my part, I pretended to be a Scot, and I put on the Scottish costume and the Scottish manner. Often when men mocked me, I shook my stick at them in the manner of the weapon called *gaveloc*, and uttered threats in the Scottish manner. When I was stopped and asked who I was, I made no answer, except [in English] "Ride, ride Rome, [re]turn Canterbury." I did this in order to conceal my design and to reach Rome safely in the Scottish disguise.

'I obtained from our Lord the pope the letter which I requested. On my return I passed a certain castle on the road which led from *Pilgrims in disguise*

Facing page A medieval town under attack. Pilgrims in these troubled times often found themselves involved in wars

Travelling through woods and countryside, pilgrims often
risked attack from bandits or hostile soldiery, but took heart

Rome: and the officers of the castle surrounded me and took me,
saying: "This vagabond, who pretends to be a Scot, is either a spy
or a messenger of the false pope Alexander." They then searched
my rags and my hose and even the old shoes which I carried on
my shoulders in the Scottish fashion.'

Samson hid the letter in a cup and they did not find it: 'They saw
the cup but not the paper. And so I escaped their hands in God's
name. But they took all the money I had, and I had to beg my way
from door to door without a penny until I reached England (19).'

By and large, however, brigandage seems to have been fairly rare,
although Margaret Paston (daughter-in-law of Agnes) wrote in
1471 to her husband John in London: 'As for my roundlet of wine,
I should send you money therefor, but I dare not put it into jeopardy,
there be so many thieves stiring.'

Thieves and   When one considers the journeys of Fabri, it is amazing that he
robbers   went so far with so little trouble from robbers. An incident on his
first return home shows that, given the choice between brigands
52   and the military, the latter was the best bet. Fabri had been left

from other martyrdoms as of St Peter Martyr in this painting
of Bellini's

behind at Venice for a fortnight because of illness, and his companions, understandably keen to get home, set out for Germany.
He then fell in with some English pilgrims who had also been to
the Holy Land. He invited them to go to Ulm with him, but they
said that they had heard that the soldiers of the Duke of Austria
were due to arrive at the inn, and they were none too happy about
the idea: 'So the inn was full of fierce men-at-arms; but when they
heard that I had come from the Holy Land they treated me with
respect as a priest and monk, and also as a soldier of the Holy
Land and the Holy Sepulchre, and invited me to say Mass for them
on the morrow, and travel with them.' They also, incidentally, paid
his bill. At the next stop they found the four English pilgrims, who
had been 'wounded, beaten, and robbed of all their property, in
the greatest sorrow and shame and wretchedness.' The pilgrims
could not have known what they were walking into, and yet it
seems foolish of them not to have taken advantage of Fabri's
offer—especially since he spoke German.

But pilgrims had to be careful. Peter Idley, in his *Instructions to*

53

Eleventh-century English carts which pilgrims and other travellers used for long journeys

Meeting strangers

his Son about 1450, says:

'Therefore with strange folk take not thy gait
At no season early nor late (20).'

Of course, a pilgrim might not have any choice in the matter.

In *The Canterbury Tales*, 'The Tale of Melibeus', Chaucer quotes the twelfth-century Spaniard Petrus Alphonsus: '... take no company by the way of a strange man, but if so be [unless it be] that thou have known him of a longer time. And if so be that he fall into thy company peradventure, without thine assent, inquire then as subtly as thou mayest of his conversation [behaviour], and of his life before, and feign thy way; say that thou wilt thither as thou wilt not go; and if he beareth a spear, hold thee on the right side, and if he bear a sword, hold thee on the left side.'

It was always possible that 'feigning the way' could make everyone lost. This did happen, as we shall see from a later example from Fabri. That time, however, it turned out to be a blessing in disguise.

Plague

There were other hazards. A plague was raging in one Dalmatian port at which Fabri's ship put in. They quickly turned about and set off for Ragusa, and just missed interception by a Turkish ship. On arrival at Rhodes, where the inhabitants had just taken off a Turkish seige, a cannon was fired at them by mistake.

Fabri knew of another hazard, not as dramatic but almost as important for the pilgrim: 'So young Master George and I, with one servant ... set forth from Memmigen ... and we and our several dispositions agreed very well together, which is a great comfort for those who are making that pilgrimage together. For if a man has a comrade with whom he cannot agree, woe betide them both during their pilgrimage!'

Rotten food

In addition to plague—which might be met anywhere in Europe then—pilgrims picked up all kinds of diseases. The *Guide du Pèlerin*

54

states quite simply: 'All fish and flesh—beef and pork—throughout Spain and Galicia make foreigners ill.'

Death frequently resulted from sickness (Fabri): '... another knight, who had gone out of his mind, expired in great pain and with terrible screams.' Even if pilgrims did not actually perish, news could get back home that they were dead. Fabri found that some Frenchmen, who had turned back at Corfu on their first trip to the Holy Land, had announced that everyone else had fallen into Turkish hands. When he returned he learned that requiems had been said for his soul!

This verse from a simple pilgrim hymn shows how familiar the pilgrim was with death:

> *'Vous qui allez à Sainct Iacques,*
> *Je vous prie humblement*
> *Que n'ayez point de haste:*
> *Allez tout bellement.*
> *Las! que les pauvres malades*
> *Sont en grand desconfort!*
> *Car maints hommes et femmes*
> *Par les chemins sont morts* (21).'

> 'You who are going to Santiago,
> I humbly beg you
> Make no haste:
> Go your way gently.
> Alas! how the poor sick folk
> Are in great discomfort!
> For many men and women
> By the wayside are dead.'

porrig carlio

5 Organisation

THE THOUSANDS who went on pilgrimage demanded that they be catered for. We have already looked at travel, and a later section will be devoted to accommodation. But other details of organisation were just as important.

First, although many pilgrims made their way by begging, most seem to have paid their way, or at least part of it. They had to carry a certain amount of money and, if they were to go abroad, make special currency arrangements. Official records of requests for travel currency give interesting figures about the numbers of pilgrims and their intended voyages.

Foreign currency

In England, Winchester Fair seems to have been the place for arranging drafts on foreign merchants for travel abroad. The fair was held each year from 1–15 September. Merchants came from abroad, or sent clerks, and had the currency ready when the pilgrim arrived on the Continent. Gerald of Barri, for example, waited at St Omer for messengers from Winchester. He had set off from Strathflur Abbey in western Wales for Rome. On his third journey, in 1203, when he arrived at Faënza he had a lot of trouble to recover the twenty gold Modenese marks which he had brought from merchants from Bologna at the Troyes fair, on his way through France. On the way back he had arranged that messengers should leave money at Troyes again for him.

It is not easy to see how much a journey cost an ordinary pilgrim, because the available records are usually those of the rich, or of officials. It has, however, been worked out that an official journey to Rome in the fifteenth century cost at least £750 in present-day terms. For the ordinary traveller, it was about £150, which still

Cost of travel

57

Facing page A merchant changing money

makes the trip a luxury by modern standards. The archives of the English Hospice in Rome show that 'pauper' guests were three times as many as the 'noble' guests who paid. Even so, there were many more visitors to Rome from England alone, so that begging must account for many more (22).

Orders of Chivalry Certain orders of knighthood were created specially to help pilgrims. In Spain the Knights of St James were attached to the shrine of Compostela. In time, the master of the order became so powerful that by the fifteenth century Ferdinand and Isabella seized the office for the crown. Another was the Order of the Holy Spirit, originally an order of hospitallers, founded by the Frenchman Guy de Montpellier in the twelfth century. In 1204 the church of Santa Maria in Saxia, Rome, was given to them by the pope; this replaced the old Schola Saxonum which had existed since the eighth century as a hospice for Anglo-Saxon travellers and pilgrims to Rome. As an order of chivalry, the Order of the Holy Spirit survived in France until the Revolution, and was to the *ancien régime* what the Order of the Garter is to the United Kingdom today.

From the thirteenth century onwards many 'confraternities' or brotherhoods were formed all over Christendom, to help pilgrims. One was at Altopascio in Tuscany, which survived until very late, and which is still recalled in the church of St Jacques du Haut-Pas in the Rue St Jacques, Paris. This church was the starting point for the Paris stage of the journey to Compostela.

Knights of Malta and Knights Templar The two most famous orders, however, are the Knights of Malta, and the Templars. The Knights of Malta began in Jerusalem in a hospital-infirmary for pilgrims founded by Blessed Gerard in the late eleventh century, before the First Crusade. Under Gerard's successor, Raymond of Provence, the order took on its military and chivalric character because of the need to defend pilgrims— and the Latin kingdom of Jerusalem—against Moslem attacks. It soon gained much property throughout Christendom, and built up a network of houses for the defence and service of pilgrims. The Templars, described by Fabri as 'most pious men, and most hospitable to pilgrims', were founded early in the twelfth century, and their seal showed a knight helping a *pauper et peregrinus* (a poor pilgrim). Their success was quick and spectacular, and in the end

Effigies of Knights Templar

led to their downfall, because of the jealousy they excited. The order was at last suppressed by Clement V in 1312, and their remaining wealth given to the Knights of Malta.

Although the orders of chivalry ran their hospices alongside those of the monastic orders, they were able to offer more physical protection to pilgrims; and as their members were not ordained (though the Templars adopted a form of the Cistercian rule), they could act as bankers, not only for pilgrims, but for kings and princes as well.

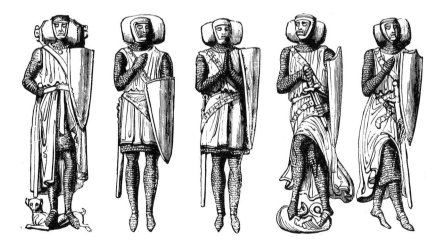

59

Perhaps the most impressive piece of pilgrim organisation was
that of the Republic of Venice. Her naval supremacy, and position
as gateway to the East, made her the natural point of departure
for pilgrims to the Holy Land by boat. In fact, Venice handled the
pilgrim traffic with all the efficiency that she brought to everything
else. Fabri learned on his second trip that a new hospice was being
entirely reserved for pilgrims on their way to Jerusalem. By then,
since 1401, there was already a system for booking passages on the
galleys: 'In this square, before the great door of St Mark's Church,
there stood two costly banners, raised aloft on tall spears, white,
and ensigned with a red cross, and they were the banners of pilgrims
to the Holy Land. By these banners we understood that two galleys
had been appointed for the transport of pilgrims; for when the
lords of Venice beheld a number of pilgrims flocking together there,
they chose two nobles from among their senators, and entrusted
the care of the pilgrims to them. The names of these were, of the
first, Master Peter de Lando, and of the second, Master Augustine
Contarini. The servants of these two noblemen stood beside the
banners, and each invited the pilgrims to sail with their master, and
they endeavoured to lead the pilgrims, the one party to the galley
of Augustine, the other to that of Peter; the one party praised
Augustine and abused Peter, the other did the reverse.'

The rivalry between the two men was intense, and although Fabri
had travelled with Contarini on the first trip, he did not want to
make his voice heard in case he were accused of bias. So he declared
that both were equally good. He decided to take the boat that was
due to sail first. But they both promised to leave at once, 'which I
knew to be a lie'. The Venetians were great salesmen. The pilgrims
were invited to look over the ships and were offered free food and
drink by each captain. In the end Fabri's party chose the larger
ship because it was also newer, and went away to draw up a long
agreement, setting out what the captain was to do for them. They
were to pay him forty newly minted ducats each, half in Venice and
half in Joppa. The captain wanted forty-five ducats and did not
want to sail for a month, proving Fabri right about their rash
promises to sail at once! But at last they hammered out a contract
acceptable to both sides, which was duly signed and sealed in the
Doge's palace. All their names were entered in a special book

(Fabri's for the second time), and a few days later they presented their letters from the Duke of Austria to the Doge in person. In return they were handed letters to the Captain-General of the Sea and the governors of the islands. At the time the Turks were chasing Venetian shipping, and Fabri and his friends were to have some narrow escapes.

Ships of St Louis of France carrying soldiers and pilgrims to the Holy Land in 1268

6 Hospices, monastic houses, inns and ships

IN THE *Guide du Pèlerin* we read: 'Three pillars—necessary above all for the sustaining of His poor people—have been established by God in this world; the hospice at Jerusalem, the hospice of Mont-Joux (the Great St Bernard) and the hospice of St Christine, on the Somport. These hospices have been installed in places where they were necessary; they are holy places, houses of God for the comfort of holy pilgrims, the repose of those therein, the consolation of the sick, the salvation of the dead and support to the living. Those who edify these holy houses will, without any doubt, and whoever they be, possess the kingdom of God.'

Three famous hospices

These hospices corresponded to the three great pilgrimages of medieval Christianity: Jerusalem, Rome and Compostela (although the hospice of St Christine was later superseded by Roncevaux). These words in the *Guide du Pèlerin* show how vital the hospices were to pilgrims. Fabri said that the Venetians were building a hospice especially for pilgrims to Jerusalem. In Rome there were two English hospices, one founded in 1362 and the other in 1396. Of the hospice at Jerusalem Fabri said: 'It used to be the custom for every pilgrim who entered the hospital to give the warden of the hospital two Venetian marks, and he had free quarters without any dispute, even if he remained in Jerusalem for a year.'

We learn more of the function of the hospice from the rule of the one at Aubrac in France, reformed by its commander, Etienne II, in the early thirteenth century. The hospice was to help pilgrims 'passing to visit the churches of our Lady of Rocamadour, Santiago, St Saviour of Oviedo and St Dominic of Estramadure, and many other saints, also those who are going to the sepulchre of our Lord.'

The hospice at Aubrac

Facing page This monk-templar still keeps his helmet and shield close by his side

Conferring the tonsure on a new monk

They must also 'receive, collect, comfort the poor, the infirm, the blind, the weak, the lame, the deaf-mutes and the hungry (23).'

Staying at monasteries Of course, monasteries also offered hospitality, and the great houses attached to Cluny made a special point of looking after them. Inns, however, were a problem, not only for pilgrims but for travellers generally. At least when he chose a ship the pilgrim could more or less see what he was in for. Unfortunately very little detailed information has survived for day-to-day life in inns and monastic houses, so we must sometimes read between the lines.

On his second journey, Fabri was very impressed with the way his party was received at the monastery of Neustift. The abbot regarded one of the noblemen in the party as his patron, so this might explain it: 'The aforesaid abbot would not let us go that day, but made us stay there, and treated us with great honour, for the

64

monastery is very grand and very rich. I have hardly anywhere seen so much gold and silver plate as in the abbot's dining-hall.'

A less grand reception, but one just as warm, was given to Fabri and his friends at Ragusa on their first journey to Jerusalem: '... we entered the city, but found no inns there as in our country. Wherefore I, with my Master George von Stein and some other noblemen, went to a convent of Dominicans, begging them to give us something to eat in return for our money. They brought us good

Left Investiture of a new abbot and *right* blessing the foundation charter of his new monastery

provisions, and capital Schavonian wine, and treated us handsomely.' Of course, they had to pay for it, and matters may well have been helped by the fact that Fabri was himself a Dominican. But one can see what a godsend the monastery was in this part of the world. In fact Fabri always felt much more at home with monks, especially the Dominicans.

We learn from Fabri's first trip to Venice how he came to choose his inn: 'On the next day ... we sold our horses, and went on mules to Margerum [Mestre?]. At Margerum we bade the land farewell, and put to sea in a barque, in which we sailed as far as Venice to the Fondaco de' Tedeschi [German Institute]. At the Fondaco itself we asked about inns for knights and pilgrims, and were taken by a certain German to the inn of St George, which is a large and respectable one.' When he arrived in Venice the second time—despite the

Staying at inns

Left A Dominican friar, *centre* a Franciscan friar, and *right* a Benedictine abbot

fact that he had stayed in that inn before—he asked to be allowed to go to a Dominican monastery. But the rest of the party would not hear of it. We are not told why, but it may be that since Fabri had been there before and was remembered by some of the Venetians, he would have been very useful to the others. In the end a compromise was reached, and a sort of cell fitted up for Fabri in the inn.

Sometimes there were no inns, as at Ragusa already mentioned. In Crete, on Fabri's first voyage, a brothel was hastily turned into an inn: 'We went into the house of a certain German, who although he kept a brothel, yet on arrival cleansed his house and sent his courtesans away; for there was no other inn there for pilgrims.'

Language difficulties When there were inns, there could be language barriers, as on Fabri's first journey, where they had made a detour. As we have seen, pilgrims sometimes lost their way: 'When we arrived at that town we found that it was Bassano, and we realised that we had gone out of our way; however, we stayed there for the night, and drank the red wine which is the speciality of the place until we were

Above A noisy supper in a fifteenth century Italian inn, and
below dinner for one in 'the House of Rest'

The houſe of reſt

The Great Bed of Ware which measured 10 feet 9 inches
square could sleep twenty people at a time

both nodding. However, we were very uncomfortable, because
there was no one in the inn who could talk German with us, and as
we knew no Italian we had to ask for everything by signs.'

At least the wine seems to have been good; but inns could be
expensive and not good, as we learn from a letter of John Paston
to his wife Margaret in 1474. He is at the George Inn, Powlys
Wharf, Southwark, London: 'And where you advised me to haste
me out of this town, I would full fain be hence. I spend daily more
than I should do, if I were hence, and I am not well purveyed.'

Trouble at   If that was all, John Paston had little to grumble about. In many
inns   ways, inns and hotels have not changed much over the last five
hundred years. Sometimes, however, more serious things happened.
Fabri had an unfortunate experience on his second journey. The
rest of the party had already left and he was trying to catch up with
them. One evening, he arrived alone at an inn: 'In the inn sat some
miners from the silver mines, who were gambling, drinking, and
taking their pleasure. I regarded them with suspicion, and was

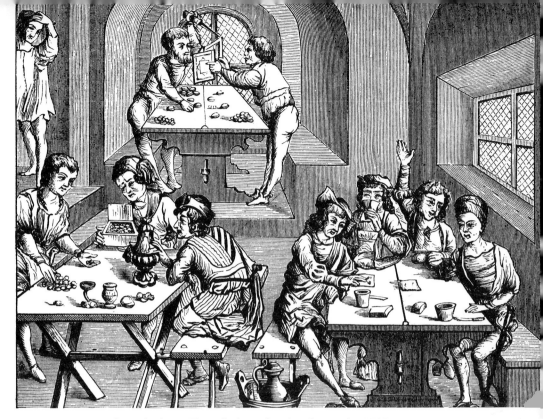

A game of cards in a French hostelry in the early 1500s

cautious in my talk with them. The landlord put me into a small room by myself where I carefully fastened the door and went to sleep.' Next day he awoke to a great commotion. The miners had robbed two carriers and made off with the money. Accommodation in inns was much more communal than it is today, to say the least. The Great Bed of Ware which could sleep twenty people may have been an exception, but large beds for poorer travellers must have been common.

There could, of course, be pleasant interludes, though even this next one caused a certain amount of heart-searching at the time: 'When it was late, and we were all sitting at supper, there came a minstrel, or *jongleur*, and his wife. He carried a flute, and his wife sang in good tune while he played his flute. This man, though he was sensible enough, made mops and mows like a fool while he was playing, which made us laugh heartily in addition to the pleasure of hearing the music.' A great discussion then arose as to whether or not they should offer him money, since they were on pilgrimage.

Entertainment

They asked Fabri to decide, and he said yes, since he was '... a mechanic dwelling in Trent, who did not make a constant practice of playing, but only on the arrival of princes or nobles; for when he heard that they were pilgrims to the Holy Land, he played for their diversion and for his own profit, in order that our sadness and anxiety might for a short time be laid aside.'

Hiring a house

If there were no local monasteries or inns, pilgrims might hire a house: 'After hearing Mass (at Corfu), we Swabian and Bavarian pilgrims hired a small cottage in the suburbs, and there cooked, ate, drank and slept. This cottage was small, and built of beams of very old and very dry wood: so it was, because of the enormous fire which we made up for cooking, that the place actually caught fire twice; however, we always put out the fire, so that we did not get into any trouble about it.'

Home cooking on an open fire

Sleeping aboard ship

Most of the details of sea travel appear in the next section, but accommodation belongs here. Medieval galleys were no luxury cruise liners. When Fabri and his companions arrived in Venice they had to choose between a brand new galley, and the older, smaller one in which Fabri had first journeyed. The party chose the larger, newer vessel. As it turned out, they might have been happier in the other

70

one. A small, irritating incident early on, in fact, set the mood for the whole trip. Whilst waiting to set sail, the pilgrims went to visit the tomb of St Helena in Venice, but on their way back to the ship found that the captain had stored planks in their quarters, which had not been there before: 'so that some of them came just by our feet where we wanted to put our shoes and chamber-pots.' After a loud argument the planks were removed. The chamber-pots evidently had other uses: 'I have seen some hot-tempered pilgrims throw their chamber-pot at burning lights to put them out.'

The passengers had to be fairly adaptable at first. Some pilgrims, fond of wine and unused to ladders, fell into the hold. On the very first night, before the ship even set sail, one of the pilgrims had a nightmare nearly leading to a riot, because of an imagined attack.

The New Inn, Gloucester, England. Built about 1450, it was much used by pilgrims travelling to the tomb of Edward II

Venice was at war with the Turks, the confusion was natural.

'Finally,' in the words of Fabri, 'among all the occupations of seafarers there is one which, though loathsome, is yet very common, daily and necessary—I mean the hunting and catching of lice and vermin. Unless a man spends several hours in this work when he is on pilgrimage, he will have but unquiet slumbers.'

71

7 En route

CONTRAST this extract from *Syr Isenbras*, an early English ballad:

> 'They bare with them no manner of thing
> That was worth a farthing
> Goods, gold nor possessions;
> But meekly they asked their meat
> Where that they might it get
> For Saint Charity (24).'

with Fabri's account of conditions on board ship when water was scarce: 'During those days I often saw these creatures [the sheep, goats, mules and pigs that they had on board] licking the planks and the spars, sucking off them the dew which had gathered in the night ... I do not tell you of the stale bread, the biscuit full of worms, the tainted meat, and the terrible cookery, all of which we should have been happy with if we had had clean water in good measure ...' But there was no lack of wine.

The extract from *Syr Isenbras* is the ideal of the pilgrim, but Fabri's shows that the pilgrim had to cope with life just like anyone else. In the eyes of some, pilgrimage was to be deplored: it seemed to be just an excuse for a break from routine. This may be true of short, local pilgrimages, but in the light of what we have now seen about pilgrimage abroad, it can hardly be true. Here is Langland in *Piers Plowman*:

Hopes and reality

> 'A host of hermits with hocked staves
> Went to Walsingham with their wenches behind them,
> These great lubbers and long, who were loath to labour,
> Clothed themselves in copes to be distinguished from others,

Piers Plowman

73

Facing page. Below 'There came at nightfall to that hostelry, Well nine and twenty in a company, Of sundry folk who by adventure fall, In fellowship, and pilgrims were they all, That towards Canterbury would ride.' *The Canterbury Tales.*

C* *Above* dicing and playing cards in a German inn

And robed themselves as hermits to roam at their leisure.
There I found friars of all the four orders,
Who preached to the people for the profit of their bellies,
And glossed the gospel to their own good pleasure;
They coveted their copes, and construed it to their liking.
Many master-brothers may clothe themselves to their fancy,
For their money, their merchandise multiply together.
Since charity has turned chapman to shrive lords and ladies,
Strange sights have been seen in a few short years.
Unless they and Holy Church hold closer together
The worst misery of man will mount up quickly.'

The four orders of friars from a thirteenth century manuscript
drawing

But Langland was a visionary, and the system he attacked was, in
effect, the whole medieval world—the world that could say:

'Ne had the apple taken been,
The apple taken been,
Ne had never our lady
A-been heavené queen.
Blesséd be the time
That apple taken was.
Therefore we moun singen
Deo gracias! (25).'

The Christian lived in a world of sin, but had a glorious redemp-
tion. In the Middle Ages, this kind of faith was perhaps the only
one possible, otherwise life would have been too intolerable for
most people.

On best   Medieval pilgrims were unashamedly earthbound, yet through
behaviour the clay glitters their faith and perseverance: '... we all decided that

no more games of cards or dice should be played on board of the galley, that no quarrels, swearing or blasphemies should be allowed, and that the clerks and priests should add litanies to their usual daily prayers ... for men were gambling morning, noon and night, especially the Bishop of Orleans with his suite ...' Langland would have been only too delighted to receive such ammunition. Gambling seems to have been a favourite occupation, because Fabri comments on it on the next journey with his German knights.

French knights of the Crusades, from a stained glass window in Chartres Cathedral

Another aspect of pilgrims' collective behaviour was the general *Rowdiness* rowdiness they were capable of, both whilst travelling and on arrival at the shrines. For St Richard's Day, 3 April 1487, Bishop Storey of Chichester had to make strict regulations. Struggles amongst pilgrims for first place in going to the shrine began to take on alarming aspects. The staves that the pilgrims carried were used as weapons, and once there had been a killing. Only banners and crosses were to be carried.

Some of the Canterbury pilgrims, *left* the miller, *centre* the
nun's priest, *right* the doctor of physic

Music   There follows a general disapproval of pilgrim habits: '... some
other pilgrims will have them baggepipes; so that everie towne
that they came through, what with the noice of their singing and
with the sound of their piping and with the jangling of their Canter-
burie bells, and with the barking out of dogges after them, that they
make more noice than if the King came there away with all his
clarions and many other minstrels (26).'

Chaucer's Miller was one of those who took along his bagpipes:

> 'A bagpipe well could he blow and sound,
> And therewithal he brought us out of town.'

And the Pardoner and Summoner used to sing duets:

> 'Full loud he sung "Come hither, love, to me".
> This Summoner bare to him a stiff bourdon [bass]:
> Was never trump of half so great a sound.'

The Pardoner, on the other hand, had a voice 'as small as hath
a goat.' The Prioress made a more pleasant noise:

> 'Full well she sang the service divine,
> Entuned in her nose full seemly ...'

As well as singing, we know from Chaucer's *Canterbury Tales*
that pilgrims often used to tell stories on the road, though of course

76

More Canterbury pilgrims, *left* the merchant, *centre* the friar,
right the squire

he was using the literary device of Boccaccio and Sercambi before
him. Here, too, Langland finds something to criticise—the practice
only leads to exaggeration and deceit:

> 'Pilgrims and Palmers were plighted together
> To seek Saint James and saints in Rome.
> They went on their way with many wise stories,
> And had leave to lie for a lifetime after.
> I saw some who said that they sought for relics;
> In each tale that they told their tongue would always
> Speak more than was so, it seemed to my thinking.'

Once they reached a town, Fabri tells us, they went to see the *Entering a*
ecclesiastical sights: 'So when we pilgrims had taken off our riding- *town*
dresses, we went to the churches to obtain indulgences ... For this
is what is done by all respectable pilgrims to Jerusalem, namely that
at whatever towns they stop on the way, they ask at once about
the churches and the relics of the saints, and visit them.'

The pilgrims did not visit these places just for their own benefit,
however. They often made undertakings for others, as Fabri
explains: 'For pilgrims to the Holy Land often carry with them to
the holy places, choice rings of gold or silver, and beads of precious
stones for "paternosters" or rosaries, or the rosaries themselves,
little gold or silver crosses, or any other precious and easily carried
trinkets, which are entrusted to them by their parents or friends,

or which they buy at Venice or in parts beyond the sea for presents to those who are dear to them; and whenever they meet with any relics, or come to any holy place, they take those jewels and touch the relics or the holy place with them, that they might derive some sanctity from the touch; and so they are returned to the friends of the pilgrim dearer and more valuable than before.'

Pilgrims as 'postmen'   Pilgrims also acted as postmen, as we learn from the Paston Letters and from an earlier source, Ramiro, a twelfth-century Maestrescula of Compostela, who wrote to St Aton, Bishop of Pistoia, and begged him to reply at once, entrusting the letter either to the Easter or—if necessary—Ascensiontide pilgrims.

Strange sights   Whilst waiting for their ship in Venice—they had to wait a month—the pilgrims decided to visit a different church each day. During his stay Fabri also saw the Corpus Christi procession, whose splendour rather shocked him, and a performing elephant. This poor elephant later had a rather unhappy career, being taken from Italy to Germany by its owner, and then on to Britain. But when a storm blew up at sea, the terrified sailors heaved the poor animal into the deep, doubtless much to its owner's grief.

A race at sea   Pilgrimages involving ship passages seem to have been more eventful than those made entirely on land. On Fabri's second trip to the Holy Land, as we have seen, there was a choice between the two ships supplied by the Venetian Republic. Actually, the journey turned into a race. By the time the ships reached Rhodes they were neck and neck. When the captain of Fabri's ship saw the other, smaller ship leave port, he at once gave orders to cast off. A trumpet was sounded to warn the passengers, but the wife of one of the pilgrims had gone to visit a church in the neighbourhood. Much to her husband's distress—but to the joy of the other passengers—she was left behind. She did not catch up with them until they were anchored off Cyprus.

Pilgrims left behind   The captain seems to have been rather hard-hearted, because he refused to take back on board two pilgrims who lacked money to go further. In the end Fabri's patrons put up the money. Since the Moslems had many ways of extracting money from Christian pilgrims, of which the captain doubtless knew, it is just possible that he was simply being realistic. However, the sight of the Holy Land made everyone join in a great thanksgiving.

Facing page A Venetian merchant ship

EUROPE AT THE TIME OF THE FIRST CRUSADES (c. AD 1100)

RUSSIA

POLAND

HUNGARY

Black Sea

EASTERN
ROMAN
EMPIRE

Constantinople

Smyrna

SELJUKID TURKEY

Rhodes

THE HOLY
LAND

Crete

CYPRUS

EAN SEA

Nazareth

Jerusalem

Bethlehem

Cairo

CALIPHATE OF CAIRO

8 Arrival and departure

IT WAS not surprising that Fabri and his fellow travellers sang *Te Deum* when they sighted the Holy Land. Yet their troubles were by no means over. Their treatment at the hands of the Moslems, even allowing for exaggeration on Fabri's part, made the overland journey to Jerusalem very uncomfortable. This was on his second journey, however, for on the first he complained that they spent only nine days in the Holy Land, 'in a great hurry, working day and night at the accomplishment of our pilgrimage, so that we were hardly given any time for rest'. It was partly this that made him want to return as soon as he could. However, this will be dealt with fully in the section devoted to Jerusalem (pp. 89–94). Here we are concerned with the more general aspects of pilgrimage, whether abroad or in one's native country.

The pilgrim's vow   The pilgrimage vow was fulfilled when the pilgrim reached the shrine and knelt in prayer and carried out his penance, if he was required to do so. The way of completing the pilgrimage to St Patrick's Purgatory on the island of Lough Derg in Ireland was rather elaborate. By 1186 the would-be pilgrim had first to be accepted by the bishop of the diocese. He then went on to Saints' Island, and after nine days was rowed to Station Island, where he spent a night and a day in the 'purgatorial cave'. He then went back to Saints' Island for nine more days of prayer and penance. The fact that there are surviving accounts from French, Hungarian and English pilgrims shows how famous and popular the place was.

Penitents   Pilgrims often assumed a penitential posture from the moment they arrived at the *mons gaudii* (*montjoie* or mountjoy), the place from which they had their first glimpse of the object of their pilgrimage; and they retained this posture until they reached their destination. Henry II did this when he went to Canterbury as a penitent to the shrine of St Thomas (page 110). At Rome, 'making the stations' was a common practice—imitating Christ's way to crucifixion. Another was mounting a staircase on hands and knees, as with the Scala Santa in Rome, the shrine on Mount Sinai and the staircase at Rocamadour in France. As a penance, pilgrims might beg at the entrance to a shrine, go round the tomb of the saint or pass under it where this was possible. Another feature was an all-night vigil in the church. Fabri and his companions spent three nights' vigil in the Church of the Holy Sepulchre.

Receiving the sacrament was naturally one of the first things a pilgrim wanted to do on arrival; there were usually plenty of confessionals, though the language barrier could present a problem. If the pilgrim came to give thanks for a cure he might bring a wax or metal model of the part of the body that had been healed, or a tablet to be placed in the church. People saved from shipwreck might bring a model of a ship, and until about 1050 the reliquary statue of St Foy at Conques in France was displayed behind a screen of chains from former prisoners, who believed they were freed by the prayers, or intercession, of the saint.

Receiving the sacrament

Usually pilgrims made gifts of money or jewellery to the shrine; oil or wax was another common gift. Fabri tells us about a church at Trent: '... people from distant parts of Germany, France and Italy make pilgrimages thither, and bring offerings of wax, clothing, gold and silver plate and money, in such quantities as is wonderful to behold. In consequence of this, they have pulled down the old church of St Peter in which the body [of the child Simeon] used to be kept, and have built a new and spacious one ...'

Gifts

As we have seen in the section on relics, most pilgrims tried to take away a relic if possible, and it seems that nearly every party that went to the Holy Land was warned against chipping away parts of altars and statues, and noblemen were asked to refrain from carving their coats-of-arms on walls and church furnishings. When Fabri and some of his party, at the conclusion of his second visit to Jerusalem, went on to St Catherine's Monastery on Mount Sinai, one of the party actually chipped off part of the altar. A message was sent from the abbot: 'A piece of the tomb of St

Stealing relics

Catharine had been broken off by an iron instrument; if we delayed to restore it, the Arabs, into whose hands he would put the matter, would see that we did so without delay.' The pilgrims tried to find the culprit: 'each one looking at another, and all cursing the man who had done it; we asked each other that the guilty party should not be ashamed to confess and give back the broken piece, and we would all share in the blame, and pay whatever was to be paid; but there was no man who would own up, till our *Calinus* said that the thief should secretly hand over to him the bit of stone, and in secrecy he would smooth the business over. And so it was done; but who among us was guilty to this day, I do not know (27).'

If a man went as far as Sinai and returned alive, he naturally wanted something to show for his pains. It seems rather strange, however, that he should have hoped to get away with so blatant a piece of vandalism.

The good of the soul There were pilgrims, however, who, as at all times, simply went for the good of their souls. Here is Roger Taverham to John Paston: 'And, sir, I suppose I shall never see you no more, nor none of mine friends, which is to me the greatest lamentation that might come into mine heart; for, sir, by the grace of God, I shall go to Rome and into other holy places to spend mine days of this present life in the service of God ...' Gerald of Barri (Giraldus Cambrensis), who had long been campaigning for a Welsh Church free from Canterbury's domination, finally failed; and to atone for all the trouble he had caused, went to Rome in 1204 as a simple pilgrim. He did not describe the journey in detail because he made it '... solely by way of pilgrimage and devotion, in order that ... by the labours of the journey, by the giving of alms, by making the stations of Rome and by earning the indulgences therefor, by true confession and at last by apostolic absolution, all the stains accumulated in his past life might be wiped away ... (28).' In this way Gerald amassed ninety-two years of indulgences, and so as to make it up to a round hundred, he became a brother in the Hospital of the Holy Spirit. In this way he obtained an indulgence of one-seventh of his sins.

The proud traveller We have already seen the description of the pilgrim from *Piers Plowman* on page 36. This pilgrim was returning, and was obviously at pains to show where he had been. This was not just for idle show, for pilgrims were anxious to make clear they were genuine. The later dialogue in *Piers Plowman* shows that, without destroying the naive sincerity of the pilgrim, there is a bitter irony in the situation, as Langland powerfully reveals:

'The folk asked him first from whence he was coming.
"From Sinai," he said, "and from our Lord's sepulchre.
In Bethlehem and Babylon [Cairo] I have been for a season;
In Armenia and Alexandria, in many other places.
You may see by the signs that stick in my hatband
How I have walked full wide in wet and dry;
I have sought good saints for my soul's welfare."
"Know you ought of a Saint whom men call Truth?
Can you put us on the path to the place where he is dwelling?"
"No, so God help me!" said this great traveller,
"I never saw a palmer, with pike and wallet,
Ask after him before, till now, at this moment."
"Peter!" cried a plowman, and put forth his shoulders,
"I know him as closely as clerk knows his lessons."'

The signs or emblems, of which there were obviously plenty in Langland's pilgrim's hat, varied from place to place. The most famous was the palm from the Holy Land—hence the term 'palmer' —and the scallop shell of St James, from the beaches of Galicia, for Compostela. Curiously enough, the sign for Rome was not the heads of the two apostles (Peter and Paul), as one might have expected, but the vernicle (veil) of St Veronica with the Holy Face. Chaucer's Pardoner wore one:

A twelfth-century pilgrim
with a scallop shell

'A vernicle had he sewn upon his cap.
His wallet lay before him on his lap,
Brimful of pardons, come from Rome all hot.'

Furthermore, the vernicle was of late date, somewhere during the fourteenth century. For Canterbury the head of St Thomas was depicted on a phial, and for Sinai a Catherine wheel recalled the martyrdom of the saint.

Long after his return, Fabri treasured his pilgrim's gown with the Jerusalem crosses on it and was very reluctant to put on the Dominican habit again. In fact, he wore a pilgrim cross under his habit for the rest of his life. To his great sorrow he also cut off the beard which he had grown for eleven months, and which he had started to grow so conscientiously when he set out to be a pilgrim for the second time.

Facing page 'Pilgrims in sight of the Holy Land', a painting of C. L. Eastlake (1783)

9 The Holy Land

PILGRIMS to Jerusalem were often known as 'palmers' because they used to bring back palms from the Holy Land. Some even branded themselves with the cross or cut themselves, as we see from *Syr Isenbras*:

> 'With a sharp knife he share [shear or cut],
> A cross upon his shoulder bare (29).'

One of the best sources for the pilgrimage to the Holy Land is that of Fabri. For one thing he was so impressed by his first visit and so regretted its brevity that he determined to return when he could. We take up the story first, however, on his first trip, when he has arrived in Venice and has been directed to an inn: 'There we found many noblemen from various countries, all of whom were bound by the same vow as ourselves, and intended to cross the sea and visit the most Holy Sepulchre of the Lord Jesus. There were also in the other inns many pilgrims, both priests, monks and laymen, gentle and simple, from Germany, from Gaul, and France, and especially two bishops, my lord of Orleans [who was a heavy gambler, as we have seen on page 75] and my lord of Le Mans, with a very large retinue of companions and attendants, were there, awaiting the sailing of a ship; and, moreover, certain women well-stricken in years, wealthy matrons, six in number, were there together with us, desiring to cross the sea to the holy places. I was astonished at the courage of these old women, who through old age were scarcely able to support their own weight, yet forgot their own frailty, and through love for the Holy Land had joined themselves to young knights and underwent the labour of strong men.

Facing page Pilgrims wind their way into fifteenth century Jerusalem. The large domed structure is the Dome of the Rock

The proud nobles, however, were not pleased at this … considering it a disgrace that they should go to receive the honour of knighthood in company with old women.' In fact the nobles seem to have been a thoroughly ungentlemanly lot, and Fabri and his friends took the old ladies into their group. Ironically, when almost everyone fell sick off Cyprus on the return home, it was the 'ancient matrons' who acted as nurses.

Fabri at sea

Fabri then tells us about the ship itself: 'Now, Master Augustine Contarini, whose name means "Count of the Rhine," a noble Venetian, was going to take a cargo of pilgrims, and we agreed with him about the fare, and hired his galley, and received from him berths and cots—that is, places for each of us to lie in the galley— and we hoped for a quick passage, for we had waited many days while the galley was being fitted for sea. But when everything was ready and there was nothing left to be done but set sail, as we longed to do, there came a ship which brought the bad news that the Emperor of the Turks, Mahomet the Great, was besieging the island of Rhodes … and that it was impossible during this year to take pilgrims across to the Holy Land.' In fact they were able to set sail after all, though they were never quite sure that the Turks would leave them alone.

Fabri and the Moslems

As to the actual arrival in the Holy Land, we learn more from Fabri's second trip, where he goes into much more detail. As we have seen on page 82, he complained that they had had to make a whirlwind tour of the Holy Land on his first trip. After the euphoria induced by sighting the Holy Land, there was a sharp contrast when the pilgrims came into contact with the Moslems. They had to spend the first night in a filthy cave, paying a Venetian penny to go in, and another to come out in the morning. This annoyed the pilgrims, but they soon grew used to this state of affairs, and accepted it as normal.

The Moslem authorities forced the two shiploads of pilgrims to go forward as one group, which annoyed the captains because of their rivalry, but the pilgrims themselves were quite happy. Fabri had, in any case, been mixing with the other party because he was planning to extend his pilgrimage to take in St Catherine's Monastery on Mount Sinai, and so wanted to sound out as many people as possible. When the captains found out they for once acted in unison, spontaneously, because they would lose twelve ducats for each pilgrim who 'defected'. They put about the story that the place had been laid waste by the Arabs; but Fabri, not surprisingly, suspected a plot, and bided his time.

Once they actually reached Jerusalem, the highpoint of the trip for the noble members of the party was the dubbing of knights in the Holy Sepulchre itself. The custom was obviously of great symbolic worth, and Fabri tells us about it in great detail: 'Now, when this procession had been formed and had been completed, and brought to an end ... this Brother John, at one hour before midnight, called together to him all the noble pilgrims who wished to receive knighthood into the church of Golgotha—that is to say, into the choir, where is the middle of the world ... and, having ranged the counts, barons, and nobles before him, began to tell them of the laws of this knighthood. In the first place he forbade that anyone should presume to come to receive this knighthood unless he be proved to be noble by four descents: of sufficient substance, just, of good report, and not disgraced by any infamous misdemeanour. He declared that should any unfit person present himself before him and be dubbed a knight, that such dubbing would be invalid, and that such a man ought not in any wise to be counted as a knight, but as a mocker and insulter and scorner of nobility. Finally, he charged them that they should draw near to receive their knight-hood in the fear of God and with reverence; that they should in all things obey the Pope and the Emperor, by whose authority this honour was conferred upon them; that they should defend the Catholic Church, and maintain its rights; that they should protect and fight on behalf of bishops, monks, all religious persons and ecclesiastics, their lands and their goods; that they should rule the commonwealth peaceably, that they should deal justly with orphans, widows, strangers, and the poor; and that they should console all faithful people in distress by affording them help when called upon. Furthermore, he forbade them to make any treaties whatsoever with the infidels, but charged them to drive them as far away from Christendom as possible, and, above all, to labour with all their strength to the end that the Holy Land and the most Holy Sepulchre might be torn from the hands of the infidels; and that they should urge upon all kings, princes, dukes, counts, marquises, and other

The dubbing of knights at Jerusalem

91

men of the sword, to come as soon as they were able to succour the Holy Land, and that they should stir up the minds of all men to help it, and should make it their business with all diligence to set forth to the faithful the piteous captivity of the Sepulchre, and that they themselves should hold themselves in readiness at all hours to set out to fight for the Holy Land.'

After this speech, the actual ceremony of dubbing was quite *The ceremony* simple: 'First, therefore, he called to him the noble Lord John, Count of Solms, into the inner cave of the Lord's monument, in which is the most holy tomb, and girded the sword of knighthood upon his thigh, tied the spurs of knighthood on his feet, and told him to bow himself down upon his bended knees before the Lord's tomb so that his knees rested upon the pavement, and his breast and arms lay upon the lid of the tomb. When he was so kneeling, this Brother John took from its sheath the sword with which the count was girded, and with its blade struck him three times upon the shoulders in the name of the Father, and of the Son, and of the Holy Spirit. After this had been done he raised up the count, loosed the sword and the spurs from him, kissed him, and respectfully said: "May it be for thy good."'

When all the knights had been dubbed, the priests said Mass, and at daybreak they all sang High Mass together 'in the sepulchre of the Lord's resurrection'. After this they waited for the Moslems to let them out. Suddenly quarrelling broke out, and it seemed that one of the party who was 'a good and merry comrade, but of too low estate to bear the dignity of knighthood' had managed to have himself dubbed. Just as Brother John had promised, he was stripped there and then of his knighthood.

It was a matter of great regret for Fabri that: 'Jerusalem ... *Moslem* continues to be held by them [the infidels] even to this day, now for *Jerusalem* three hundred years down to this our own unhappy time. Well may I call this time of ours unhappy, in which the evening of faith hath drawn in upon the world, and the chaos and night of wickedness abounds.' Of course this was a most appropriate place for Fabri to indulge himself, and it is also traditional—if not specially appropriate—for writers of this sort to lament their own time. Actually, Fabri was being prophetic, because the troubles that were about to be unleashed on the Church in Europe would make people leave

93

Facing page A crusading knight praying

Jerusalem to its own devices for many years to come.

Fabri sums up   Let us leave Jerusalem with Fabri's conclusion to his first journey to the East: 'By this all men may see clearly how untrue is the common saying, that the pilgrimage by sea from Venice to the Holy Land is a mere pleasant excursion with little or no danger … It required courage and audacity to attempt this pilgrimage. That many are prompted to it by sinful rashness, and idle curiosity, cannot be doubted; but to reach the holy places and to return to one's home active and well is the especial gift of God.'

10 Rome

THE PILGRIMAGE to Rome gave a new word to the English language —'roam'—and the pull of Rome for pre-Reformation England should not be underestimated. The tradition for voyages to Rome began early on, and is recorded by Bede, in his *History of the English Church and People*. We read of Caedwalla, King of the West Saxons, who died towards the end of the seventh century: '[He] abdicated from his throne for the sake of our Lord and his eternal kingdom, and travelled to Rome. For having learned that the road to heaven lies open to mankind only through baptism, he wished to obtain the particular privilege of receiving the cleansing of baptism at the shrine of the blessed Apostles. At the same time, he hoped to die shortly after his baptism, and pass from this world to everlasting happiness [not the first, or last, deathbed conversion]. By God's grace, both of these hopes were realised. Arriving in Rome during the pontificate of Sergius, he was baptised on Holy Saturday before Easter in the year of our Lord 689, and fell ill while still wearing his white robes. He departed this life on 30 April, and joined the company of the blessed in heaven (30).'

Benedict Biscop (628–89) made five journeys to Rome, during which he brought back several books of immense value to the Church in England. Wilfrid of York (634–709) was another traveller to Rome, making two journeys.

Matthew Paris attributed to King Ina of Wessex (Caedwalla's successor) the foundation of the famous Schola Saxonum (Saxon Hostel) in Rome. From Bede we learn that he too abdicated and went to Rome: 'Having ruled the nation for thirty-seven years, Ina also abdicated, and handed over the government to younger men.

'Roaming'

Caedwalla

Benedict Biscop

King Ina

95

He then set out to visit the shrines of the blessed Apostles during the pontificate of Gregory [II], wishing to spend some of the time of his earthly pilgrimage in the vicinity of the holy places, hoping thereby to merit a warmer welcome from the saints in heaven. At this period, many English people followed this custom, both noble and simple, layfolk and clergy, men and women alike (31).'

All Europe in Rome This must be true for all the countries which adopted the Christianity of Rome. The Franks had their church of St Saviour in Rome, the Frisians, St Michael, and the Lombards, St Justin. Hospitals were often attached to these churches, and so they became little enclaves within the city of Rome. The Anglo-Saxon colony around the Schola Saxonum and the church of Santa Maria in Trastevere gave its name to the *borgo*. Later, Leo III dedicated a pilgrim hostel, which he founded in Rome, to St Peregrinus of Auxerre.

The first Holy Year This practice grew in importance, but what really gave impetus to the pilgrim traffic was the declaration by Boniface VIII of the first Holy Year in 1300. In that year, the population of Rome is estimated to have been a steady 200,000 above normal. Further jubilee years followed in 1350 (Clement VI), 1390 (Urban VI), 1400 (Boniface IX), 1423 (Martin V), 1450 (Nicholas V), and then every twenty-five years down to the present day. In holy years a solemn plenary indulgence (see pp. 29–30) is granted to the faithful when they have fulfilled certain requirements, and special conditions come into force for confessors. Dante, in the *Inferno* (XVIII, 28–33) refers to the two streams of pilgrims on the Sant'Angelo bridge for the celebrations of 1300. For that of 1450, 40,000 people were said to arrive daily.

Pilgrim tour of Rome The pilgrim circuit at Rome is set out by Adam of Usk at the start of the fifteenth century: 'The circuits of full indulgence, to lighten the heavy toil of visiting others, are confined to seven churches: to wit, St John Lateran, St Mary the Greater, St Cross of Jerusalem, St Peter, St Paul, St Lawrence without the walls, and SS Fabian and Sebastian. Also, since it would be too much labour to visit all places of indulgence in the church of St Peter [the Vatican], it sufficeth to visit within the circuit seven altars: to wit, the greater altar of St Peter, wherein he lieth, as too St Paul doth in the greater altar of his church, although their heads are in St John Lateran, adorned with gold; also the altars of St Cross, St Veronica, St Gregory, SS Fabian and Sebastian, St Leo, pope, and St Andrew (32).'

In another early guide book, *De locis sanctis martyrum quae sunt foris civitatis Romae*, although the visit begins at St Peter's, the other places visited are all outside the city. In his *History of the English Kings*, William of Malmesbury (d.1142) preserves a much older itinerary of Rome which led the pilgrim out of fourteen gates in the Aurelian Wall to visit all the cemeteries between the Porta Cornelia and the Porta Flaminia. Matthew Paris's map itinerary (1253) in the British Museum, London, shows a journey to the Holy Land which takes seven weeks from England to Rome.

It is interesting to see just what sort of legends were told to gullible pilgrims. In St Peter's stood an altar supposed to have been built by St Peter himself; on the way to Ostia was an oratory with a stone on the altar, and the stone was said to have been used in the stoning of St Stephen; in the porch of St Lawrence's Church was the rock supposed to have drowned St Abundus; in Santa Maria in Trastevere was a portrait of Our Lady painted by herself; other items on show in Rome were the chains of St Peter and St Lawrence's gridiron. *Gullible pilgrims*

For an interesting account of a visit to Rome in the mid-fourteenth century, from a manuscript in Corpus Christi College, Cambridge, let the author speak for himself: 'On the 8th [18th] November in the above year [1344] we came to Rome, and went incontinent to the church of St Peter, the mistress of all churches, which is beyond the Tiber in a corner, as it were, of the city, in a certain high place. The ascent is by many steps, the entrance by a door, and there is a certain large space [or court], and in the middle is the top of the round temple (once called Pantheon, now St Mary Rotunda): that top of bronze in the shape of a pine-cone was carried off there by the devil on the night on which the Virgin brought Christ into the world. Then we went on and entered a certain court before the doors of the church which are sumptuously constructed, and there sit sellers of jewels: and then lie open the doors to the church which is the largest of all churches in the world: with five roofs and four rows of columns, 100 feet wide, and as long as a crossbow will shoot, as I figure, and with many chapels on the side. If one loses his companion in that church, he may search for a whole day, *A visit to Rome*

97

Pages 98 and 99 A plan of Rome in the time of Pope Clement XIII, showing the seven churches of the City

Nº 8.
S. Laurentii Basilica extra Muros
in Via Tiburtina   a Constantino
Magno Imperatore   edificata.

Nº 7.
Ecclesia Sanctæ Crucis in
Hierusalem a Constantino Filio
magni Constantini edificata.

Lateranensis Basilica S
Cælium in suo Palatio a
    Imperatore   e

Basilica S. Petri in Vati
    Imperatore

Nº 9.
Basilica S. Mariæ Majoris a Ioannes Patritio
Romano et conjuge sua edificata ob miraculum
Nivis in die quinta Augusti.

Castrum   Sancti Angeli.

PONT OPT MAX

N.º 4.
Ecclesia S. Mariæ ab
Angelo Salutatæ.

N.º 5.
S. Sebastiani Ecclesia extra muros
in Via Appia a S. Lucina ædificata
in Locum hujus ecclesiæ Sixtus V. ecclesiam
S. Mariæ Populi substituit.

N.º 3.
Ecclesia sanctorum Vicentii
et Anastasii ad tres fontes.

Lavacrum Constantini.

...nes super Montem
...antino Magno
...ta

N.º 2.
Basilica S. Pauli a Magno
Constantino Imperatore ædificata.

...a Constantino Magno
...ædificata.

Pons Sixti

Pons S Bartholomei

R

F

L

U

M

E

Pons S. Mariæ

P. Pinciana

P. Salaria

Appia

P. Maior

S. Praxis

P. Latina

P. Populi

P. S. Sebastiani

Pons S Ang.

P. S. Pauli

because of its size and because of the crowds who run from place to place, venerating shrines with kisses and prayers, since there is no altar at which indulgence is not granted.'

He goes on to speak of the classical remains: 'For I believe that on the city and its inhabitants has fallen the curse of the prophet, speaking in the name of the Lord, and saying, Confounded be all they that serve graven images, that boast of idols (Psalm 97.7); and again, They that make them are like unto them: so is everyone that trusteth in them (115.8). The women of the city are very devout, and friendly to pilgrims, but the men are crafty, Who rejoice to do evil, and delight in the frowardness of the wicked (Proverbs 2.14) (33).'

Here is an account of the indulgences and churches of Rome from the time of Brother Fabri, the last decades of the fifteenth century: 'The first church, of the Lateran, was dedicated by St Silvester pope in honour of the Holy Saviour and of St John Baptist and Evangelist; and there are in that church every day forty-eight years of indulgences and forty days, and the remission of one-third of all sins. Pope Silvester, and Gregory who consecrated it, gave so many indulgences that only God can count them, according to St Benedict, who says: if men knew of the indulgences at the Lateran church, they would not need to go by sea to the Holy Sepulchre or to St James in Galicia. Also pope Boniface says: whoever comes to our seat at the Lateran for devotion, prayer or pilgrimage, he will be absolved of all his sins. Also, in the sacristy of the same church, is the altar which St John had in the desert. Also there is the ark of the covenant of the Old Testament. Also the table on which our Lord Jesus Christ supped with his disciples. Also the rod of Moses and Aaron. All these things were carried away from Jerusalem by Titus and Vespasian [after its fall in AD 70], together with the four bronze columns which stand above the high altar. Also, above the high altar, are the heads of St Peter and St Paul, and whenever they are shown, there are as many indulgences as at St Peter's when the shroud of Veronica is shown; these indulgences on the showing of the veronica will be listed in the following ages in the mention of the second principal church (34).'

We see why the vernicle was more popular as a pilgrim emblem than the heads of the Apostles, if the number of indulgences was

the same for both. Also, one must bear in mind that the vernicle
bore the imprint of our Lord's face, as indeed the Holy Shroud
bears the imprint of His body. When the latter was exhibited at
Trier in 1512, 100,000 people are said to have gathered there.

A view of Rome from St Peter's, showing the Vatican Library

11 Santiago de Compostela

PILGRIMAGES to Compostela might be imposed as a sacramental penance (see page 18) or as a punishment by a judge (see page 20). From North and Central France three great pilgrims' roads led from Le Puy, Vézelay and Orléans. St Denis, Paris and Chartres were starting points for those coming from farther north; and for those coming by ship from England, Normandy· and Brittany, the port of Soulac, on the peninsula above Bordeaux, was another means of access. All these routes met at Saint-Jean Pied-du-Port, and then via Cise and Roncevaux (Roncesvalles) entered Spain. In Puenta la Reina this route was joined by the road from Arles via Toulouse, Col de Somport and Jaca.

In the *Codex of Santiago*, St Foy of Conques is recognised as the twelfth station on the road to Compostela, for pilgrims coming from Germany or Burgundy by way of Le Puy. Along the routes we see the similarity of ground plan between St Foy of Conques, St Sernin of Toulouse and the basilica of Santiago itself; also with two churches now no longer in existence, St Martial of Limoges and St Martin of Tours. The question of where the original inspiration came from is complicated. Certainly, the ambulatories in the apses of these great churches made the movement of pilgrims easier, but we should in any case refer back to the basilica at Bethlehem and that of the Holy Sepulchre itself for the real source of inspiration.

We have already listened to Aimery Picaud in his *Guide du Pèlerin* about road conditions (pages 42–4), and about hospices and inns (page 63). Now let us see what he has to say about the rest of the journey and Santiago itself: 'On leaving this country (Gascony), the road of St James crosses two rivers that flow near

103

Facing page A decorated portico of the Cathedral of Santiago de Compostela in Spain

the village of Saint-Jean de Sorde, one to the right and the other to the left; one is called "torrent", the other "river"; it is impossible to cross them by any means other than a boat. May their boatmen be cursed! In fact, although these rivers are quite narrow, these people still demand from each person they take over to the other side, rich and poor alike, a coin, and one for a horse; they unworthily exact by force, four! Now their boat is small, made out of a single tree trunk, scarcely able to take the horses; Also, when you get in, take care not to fall into the water. You would be well advised to hold your horse by the bridle, behind you, in the water, out of the boat, and only get in yourself with a few passengers, for if the boat is too loaded, it keels over immediately. Several times also, having taken the money, the ferrymen let such a large number of pilgrims on that the boat turns over and the pilgrims are drowned; and then the boatmen rejoice wickedly, after recuperating the corpses.'

Picaud then comes to the Basque country: 'In this country are bad toll-officials, namely in the ports of Cize, in the town called Ostabat, at Saint-Jean and Saint-Michel Pied-de-Port; quite frankly they should be sent to the devil. They come out in front of pilgrims with two or three staves, to exact an unjust tax by force, and if any traveller refuses to yield to their demand and give money, they strike him with their staves and take the money from him, cursing him and searching him down to his breeches. They are fierce people and the land they live in is also hostile with its forests and its wildness; the fierceness of their faces and apparently that of their barbarous speech, frightens the hearts of those who see them. Although they ought not regularly demand a tax from any other than single merchants, they do so unjustly on pilgrims and all travellers. When custom requires that they claim four or six pennies as duty on an object, they take eight or twelve, in other words, double.'

Picaud then demands that all the local magnates responsible for this state of affairs be excommunicated until they have done public penance and, more important, moderated the taxes they impose on travellers.

Port de Cize   He then goes on to mention Port de Cize, with its cross, known as the Cross of Charles, because: 'it is at this point that with axes, picks, pickaxes and other instruments, Charlemagne, going into

Spain with his armies, once made his way and erected first, symbolically, the Lord's cross and then bending the knee, turned towards Galicia and offered a prayer to God and to St James. Also, once they reach this spot, the pilgrims habitually genuflect and pray, turning towards the country of St James, and each one plants his cross like a standard. You may find up to a thousand crosses there. That is why this place is the first station for prayer on the way of St James.'

Much of the narrative about Santiago de Compostela itself is *The basilica* devoted to a minute description of the basilica: 'There will be nine towers in this church: two over the fountain [north] portal and two over the southern door; two over the west door and two over either spiral staircase, and the tallest will be over the crossing in the middle of the basilica. By virtue of this and the other very beautiful details of its work, the basilica of Santiago is resplendent with glory. It is entirely built of very solid stone, brown and as hard as marble; inside it is decorated with various paintings, and on the outside perfectly covered with tiles and lead. But of all of which we have just spoken, a part is completely finished, another still to finish.'

Now Picaud comes to the shrine itself: 'Until now we have spoken *The shrine* of the characteristics of the church, now we must deal with the venerable altar of the apostle. In this venerable basilica rests, according to tradition, the revered body of St James above the high altar, magnificently raised in his honour; it is enclosed in a tomb of marble sheltered by a very fine vaulted sepulchre of admirable work and convenient dimensions. It is certain that his body is fixed there, never to be moved, if one believes the witness of St Théodemir, bishop of this town, who once found it and never came to move it. May the rivals beyond the mountains [the Pyrenees] be confounded, who pretend to have some fragments and relics of him. In fact the apostle's body is here in its entirety, the body divinely illuminated by heavenly carbuncles, ceaselessly honoured by sweet, divine odours, embellished by the radiance of celestial torches and surrounded by the cares of attentive angels.'

Picaud then gives the exact measurements of the altar and its frontal, in case anyone should want to make a gift of an altar cloth or frontal. If so, he will not need to go to Compostela first. Another gift to the cathedral, much more mundane, but much more necessary

A pilgrim asking for bread and water at a wayside house

whilst it was being built, were the pieces of limestone that the pilgrims picked up near Triacastela and then took to Compostela, where there was no limestone; it provided mortar for the building.

Local people In the *Guide du Pèlerin* two stories show what happens to those who deny food and shelter to pilgrims to Compostela. These are doubtless all part of pilgrimage folklore, but they would both warn those who thought of ignoring the pilgrims, and give comfort to the pilgrims themselves: 'In Villeneuve, a poor pilgrim to Santiago went up to a woman who had some bread under hot ashes and asked her for alms for the love of God and Blessed St James; she replied that she had no bread, to which the pilgrim replied "May it please heaven that your bread turn to stone." And the pilgrim left the house and was already a long way off when this wicked woman, going to the ashes to take her bread, only found there a round stone. With a contrite heart she at once set out in search of the pilgrim, but could not find him.'

Or again, this time in Poitiers, where two penniless pilgrims returning from Compostela tried a whole street of houses before they were finally offered lodging. During the night all the houses in that street were burned down, apart from the one in which the pilgrims had spent the night. 'That is why everyone should know that, rich or poor, pilgrims of Santiago are entitled to hospitality and a welcome full of attentions.'

Compostela was a favourite pilgrimage for English people. In 1395, six hundred pilgrims left Bristol by ship, and in the next century a guide book was published entitled *The Way from the Lond of Engelond unto Sent Jamez in Galiz*. In 1428 permission was given to 916 people to go on pilgrimage to Compostela, and in 1434, 2,460. A curious law remained for a long time on the statute book, giving the Keeper of the Tower of London the right to levy sixpence on every English traveller to Compostela. The Constitutions of the University of Salamanca of 1422 show that professors might be excused from lecturing for *peregrinationes ad limina Sancti Jacobi*, pilgrimages to Compostela. Chaucer's Wife of Bath, as well as her other pilgrimages, had been to Compostela: *English visitors*

> 'And thrice had she been at Jerusalem;
> She had passed many a strange stream;
> At Rome she had been, and at Boulogne,
> In Galicia at Saint-James, and at Cologne.'

Even Brother Fabri found time for a pilgrimage to Compostela, but it did not, unfortunately, inspire him to write about it, as he did about Jerusalem and Sinai.

12 Canterbury and other places of pilgrimage

THERE were literally hundreds of places of pilgrimage before the Reformation. To list them all would need a book in itself. Yet some must be mentioned, as they were extremely important.

From the registers of the Inquisition at Carcassonne we learn that the great pilgrimages, imposed as penances for more serious crimes, were: the tomb of the Apostles at Rome, Santiago de Compostela, St Thomas of Canterbury, and the relics of the Three Kings at Cologne. Cologne, as we saw at the end of the previous section, was one of the places visited by Chaucer's Wife of Bath.

From the sixth century, because of an apparition, Monte Gargano in Apulia was dedicated to St Michael, patron saint of Europe; after Mont Saint-Michel was built in France in 710, however, the latter became the more important for St Michael. Subiaco, for its associations with St Benedict, is described by Petrarch as : '... that terrible and devout cavern which those who have seen it think they have seen the very threshold of Paradise.' Montecassino had similar popularity. The House of the Virgin at Loreto had a phenomenal success. It was actually started in 1295, but was really only brought to public attention by a papal bull of 1491. William Wey, in his *Itineraries* of 1462, describes it as: '... a villa twelve miles hence from Ancona and three from Reconato, which is called Loreta, where now is the stone chapel of St Mary, once in the Holy Land, built by St Helena. The chapel was lifted by angels, the blessed Virgin sitting on it, and transported from the Holy Land to Alreto [*sic*] in sight of farmers and shepherds (35).'

St Michael

St Benedict

The most spectacular rise in popularity came to the shrine of St Thomas at Canterbury. The cult of the saint himself did, of course,

St Thomas of Canterbury

Facing page The martyrdom of St Thomas à Becket at Canterbury Cathedral, from an illumination drawn a few years after the event

rise dramatically. Thomas was murdered on 29 December 1170, and on 21 February 1173 he was canonised by Pope Alexander III. But even in the year following his death the cult began, and as an English place of pilgrimage Canterbury was only surpassed by Walsingham at the end of the fifteenth century, and shortly before its desecration by Henry VIII.

On 12 July 1174 Henry II did public penance for his part in the murder of Becket. Roger of Howden wrote: 'Henry set out on a pilgrimage to the tomb of Saint Thomas the martyr, Archbishop of Canterbury. As soon as he neared the city, in sight of the Cathedral in which lay the body of the blessed martyr, he dismounted from his horse, and having taken off his shoes, with bare feet and dressed in [rough] woollen garments, he walked three miles to the tomb of the blessed martyr, with such meekness and repentance that it really may be held to have been the work of Him who looketh down on the earth and maketh it to tremble. To those who saw them, his footsteps seemed to be covered in blood, and so it really was; for his tender feet were cut by the hard stones, and much blood flowed from them to the ground. When he arrived at the tomb, it was a reverent sight to see how he submitted himself to the discipline of the bishops and many of the priests and monks (36).'

Henry also promised to go to the Crusades for three years and to keep a regiment of Knights Templars in the field at his expense for a year. Such was Becket's popularity that he appeared in the Byzantine mosaics at Monreale in Palermo, Sicily, which were made between 1174 and 1182. Henry II's daughter, Joan, married William the Good of Sicily in 1177. At Sens there is a high relief that dates from the late twelfth century, and Becket's vestments are kept there. Also from the late twelfth century are a font at Lyngsjo in Sweden and a fresco in SS Giovanni e Paolo at Spoleto, Italy. Also in Italy is a thirteenth-century fresco at Subiaco.

Roger of Howden tells us about another royal visitor to Canterbury. On 23 August 1179 Louis VII, who had befriended Becket during his stay in France, came to pray for the good health of his son, Philip Augustus, who had fallen seriously ill: '... upon his arrival, Louis, King of the Franks, offered upon the tomb a golden cup of great size and immense value; further he also dedicated, for the use of the monks of the church, a hundred tuns of wine to be

110

Facing page Three scenes from the life of Thomas à Becket, *top* receiving his appointment as Chancellor, *centre* his consecration as Archbishop of Canterbury, and *below* Becket reproving Henry II

delivered to them each year, for ever, at Poissy, in France, at the absolute expense of the King of France. Again, he granted to them, and all their goods or material which they henceforth purchased in France for their own use, freedom from all tolls and customs duties ... Meantime, his son Philip, by the merits and prayers of the blessed Saint Thomas the Martyr, was restored to his former health (37).'

In 1185 came Heraclius, Patriarch of Jerusalem, on his way to persuade Henry to go on a Crusade. With him were the Grand Masters of both the Templars and the Hospitallers, though the former had died on the way.

Translation of relics to a new resting place, from a drawing by Matthew Paris

Translation of St Thomas' relics

Probably the most splendid and solemn occasion that Canterbury saw, however, was on 7 July 1220. On that day, the relics of St Thomas were 'translated'—removed from their resting place in the crypt—into the great shrine that had been prepared behind the present high altar, fifty years after the saint's martyrdom. The translation had been announced two years earlier, so that everyone could come who wished to. Indulgences were granted to all those who came to Canterbury within the next twenty-five days. They were also forgiven forty days of any penance they happened to be undergoing at the time. The papal legate then granted another forty days, and so did the three archbishops present. Each of the bishops present granted twenty days, so that in all it was possible to gain 540 days of indulgence.

For the jubilee of St Thomas, in 1370, many people took to the road, and there was free food and drink for the asking all the way from London to Canterbury. Simon Sudbury, then Bishop of London and later Archbishop of Canterbury, overtook a large group of pilgrims on the London Road: 'Plenary indulgence for your sins by repairing to Canterbury? Better hope might ye have of Salvation had ye stayed at home and brought forth fruits meet for repentance!'

A Kentish squire, Thomas of Aldon, replied: 'My lord Bishop, for that you have thus spoken evil of St Thomas and are minded to stir up the minds of the people against him, I will give up mine own salvation if you yourself do not die a most shameful death (38).' Sudbury was beheaded eleven years later on Tower Hill.

The badge of a Canterbury pilgrim showing the face of Thomas à Becket

The relics at Canterbury

If the body of St Thomas were not enough, there were several other relics to be seen at Canterbury: the whole arms of eleven saints, including those of St Gregory, St Mildred the Virgin and St Hugh of Lincoln; the heads of St Blasius, St Fursaeus and St Austroberta; part of the arm of St Jerome and a piece of the arm of St Paulinus, the bed of the Blessed Virgin Mary and wool of her own weaving; a fragment of the rock on which the Cross stood, a piece of rock from the Holy Sepulchre, others from the manger, the column at which our Lord was scourged and the stone on which He stood before His Ascension. Aaron's rod, and a piece of the clay from which Adam was made, completed the list.

The tomb of St Thomas

The showing of the shrine itself was carefully stage-managed. In flickering candlelight, to the tinkling of little bells, the cover over the shrine was slowly raised. A monk then pointed out the various bequests, their givers, origins and values, with a white wand, and

113

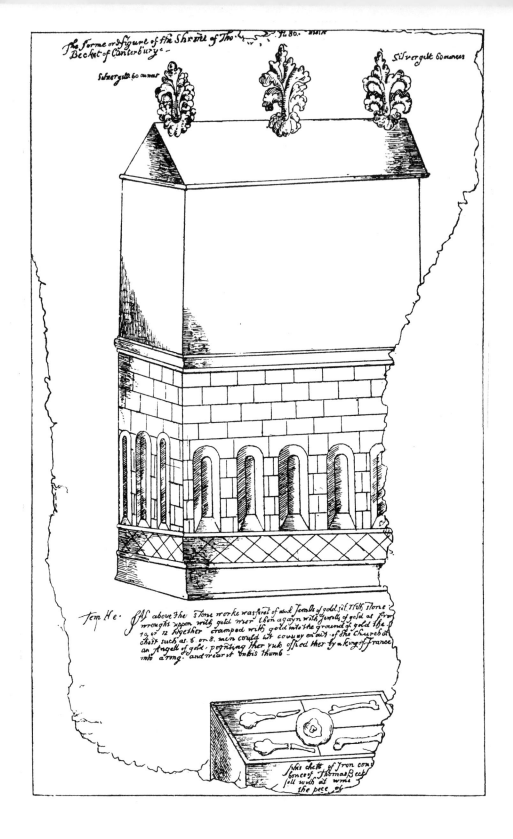

The forme or figure of the Shrine of Tho. Becket of Canterbury.

fl. 80.

Silver gilt. 60 ownas

Silver gilt 60 ownces

Item He. As above The stone worke was first of deal, Jewells of gold set with stone
wrought uppon with gold wer then agayn with Jewells of gold as for
10 or 12 together cramped with gold into the ground of gold the
chest such as 6 or 8 men could lett convay on aiste of the Church at
an Angell of gold, poynting ther vuto offred ther by a king of france
into a ring and wear it on his thumb

this chest of Iron con
bones of Thomas Beck
fell with at wme
the pece of

the cover was lowered again. Doubtless through such a dazzling and fleeting vision of the wealth of this world the pilgrim went away with some sense of the otherworldly riches enclosed within—the glorious relics of St Thomas.

About 1500 the following description of the shrine was given by an anonymous Venetian: 'The tomb of St Thomas the Martyr excels all belief. Notwithstanding its great size, it is wholly covered with plates of pure gold, yet the gold is scarcely seen because it is covered with various precious stones, as sapphires, balasses,

A glass-painting of Becket's shrine at Canterbury in the thirteenth century

diamonds, rubies and emeralds; and wherever the eye turns something more beautiful than the rest is observed. Nor, in addition to these natural beauties, is the skill of art wanting, for in the midst of the gold are the most beautiful sculptured gems, both small and large, as well as such as are in relief, as agates, onyxes, cornelians and cameos; and some cameos are of such size that I am afraid to name it; but everything is far surpassed by a ruby, not larger than a thumb-nail, which is fixed at the right of the altar. The church is

115

Facing page A very early manuscript sketch of the shrine of Thomas à Becket at Canterbury

A manuscript illumination of pilgrims travelling to Canterbury

somewhat dark, and particularly in the spot where the shrine is placed, and when we went to see it the sun was near setting; nevertheless, I saw that ruby as if I had it in my hand. They say that it was given by a King of France (39).' Little did this Venetian observer know that the shrine was near the sunset of its life, too, and that the ruby would soon adorn the person of Henry VIII.

The last recorded visit to Canterbury came in August 1538, when Madame de Montreuil was on her way back to France from Scotland. The Prior of Canterbury offered her the head of St Thomas, but she refused either to kneel to it or to kiss it. 'So she departed and went to her lodging to dinner. And about four of the clock, the said Prior did send her a present of coneys, capons, chickens, with diverse fruits—plenty—insomuch that she said, "What shall we do with so many capons? Let the Lord Prior come and help us eat them to-morrow at dinner," and so thanked him heartily for the said present (40).' As Madame de Montreuil and the Prior of Canterbury consumed their capons, the curtain fell for the last time on the shrine of St Thomas.

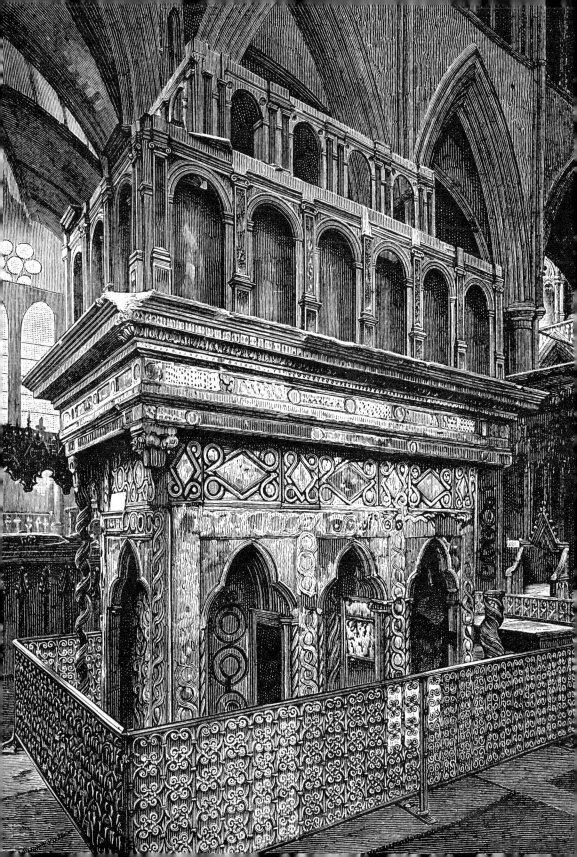

Epilogue

AS SIR Steven Runciman declares at the end of his great work on the Crusades: 'The Crusades were launched to save Eastern Christendom from the Moslems. When they ended the whole of Eastern Christendom was under Moslem rule. When Pope Urban preached his great sermon at Clermont the Turks seemed about to threaten the Bosphorus. When Pope Pius II preached the last Crusade the Turks were crossing the Danube . . . Seen in the perspective of history the whole Crusading movement was a vast fiasco ... For three centuries there was hardly a potentate in Europe who did not at some time vow with fervour to go on the Holy War. There was not a country that failed to send soldiers to fight for Christendom in the East. Jerusalem was in the mind of every man and woman. Yet the efforts to hold or recapture the Holy City were peculiarly capricious and inept (41).'

As Runciman goes on to show, politics was possibly the only sphere in which the Crusades made any impact on the history of the western world. The absence of the warlords in the East facilitated the rise of independent monarchs in the West, to the final disadvantage of the Papacy. In time, the tendency for these monarchs to set up their own national churches severely cut into the temporal power of the papacy, to the point where it has more or less disappeared today.

Pilgrimages to the Holy Land were neither more easy nor more difficult than they had been before the Crusades were inaugurated. What made a vast difference was the state of Europe itself. Dynastic wars in France and Italy, as well as religious wars; the revolt of the Low Countries and the Thirty Years' War in Germany; all plunged

119

Facing page A famous English shrine, that of Edward the Confessor at Westminster Abbey, London. It is seen as restored after 1556

Europe into a long period of uncertainty and hardship. The suppression of monastic houses made would-be pilgrims think twice before setting out. But more than that, the spirit of the age was against them.

The Reformation There is a school of thought which attributes the whole 'Reformation' to social and political causes; and there are undeniably elements of both which greatly influenced the course of events.

Three leading figures of the Reformation, from left to right, Erasmus, Luther, and John Knox

Emergent nationalism, the rise of independent monarchies, was certainly another highly important factor. But to ignore the unquenchable flame of religious reform is to look through completely the wrong end of the telescope.

There was a real desire for reform amongst Christians. Some wanted to see this happen within the old framework of medieval religion, and thought it perfectly possible. Others, however, thought that radical change was the only possible course of action. It was unfortunate that religious practices came to be identified with nationalist or dynastic hopes. One only has to look at the course of

120

the religious wars in France, or the way in which the break with Rome was brought about in England, to see the truth of this. People found themselves forced to take sides, or driven into doctrinal positions which they hardly understood. Henry VIII is credited with making the break with Rome—for dynastic purposes. Yet his doctrinal position was basically orthodox; so much so that the pope gave him the title of Defender of the Faith—*Fidei defensor*

The printing presses of the Renaissance played a major part in destroying the old medieval order

—a title still born by English monarchs, and still appearing on coins of today.

Whether it would have been possible to bring reform without breaking up Christendom is a moot point. The weight of the evidence seems to imply not. Too much had happened, Renaissance man was too aware of himself to go on in the same old way. One can accuse the papacy at this period of having been terribly short-sighted. Although most popes of the time were essentially products of the Renaissance, they were still using medieval methods—such as indulgences—to run the Church. Of course, one can argue that they were dealing with people who were mostly still medieval in outlook, but such a policy merely speeded up the discrediting of the Church in the eyes of those most able to help it.

Erasmus and Calvin   A man like Erasmus could see that beneath the layers of super-stition and trafficking was genuine piety. Others, like Calvin, were less patient. In his *Treatise on Relics* (1543) Calvin vehemently denounced the 'anthill of bones' revered by the faithful. He found as much wood of the supposed True Cross 'as to make a full load for a good ship', or again, thorns of the Crown of Thorns in such number that 'it must have been a hedge, there are so many churches that have them'.

Had pilgrimages not been so much part and parcel of the relics and the indulgences, it is possible that they might have survived with less change. As it is, they have survived in a very different form, and some that had been discontinued have even been revived. The spirit of pilgrimage is by no means dead in the Church yet. T. S. Eliot wrote in *Murder in the Cathedral*:

'... wherever a saint has dwelt, wherever a martyr has given his blood
   for the blood of Christ,
There is holy ground, and the sanctity shall not depart from it,
Though armies trample over it, though sightseers come with guide-
   books looking over it;
From where the western seas gnaw at the coast of Iona,
To the death in the desert, the prayer in forgotten places by the broken
   imperial column,
From such ground springs that which forever renews the earth
Though it is forever denied ... (42).'

Picture Credits

Sources

(1) S. Runciman, *A History of the Crusades*, I, 3 (Cambridge, 1951)

(2) R. Thurneysen, *Old Irish Reader* (Dublin, 1949), translated by D. A. Binchyard O'Bergin

(3) J. Bromyard, *Summa Praedicantium* (Lyons, 1522), quoted in *Catholic Encyclopedia* (New York, 1907–14), article on 'Pilgrimage'

(4) B. Thorpe, *Ancient Laws* (London, 1840)

(5) *The Paston Letters*, edited by J. Gairdner (London, 1904), the spelling modernised by the author of the present work

(6) *La Vita Nuova*, translated by D. G. Rossetti (Portland, Maine, 1896)

(7) *New Catholic Encyclopedia* (New York, 1967), article on 'Pilgrimage'

(8) *Ibid.*, article on 'Indulgences'

(9) All the quotations from *The Canterbury Tales* are taken from *The Complete Works of Geoffrey Chaucer*, edited by F. N. Robinson, 2nd ed. (Oxford, 1957), the spelling modernised by the author of the present work

(10) All the quotations from *Piers Plowman* are from the translation by H. W. Wells (London, 1935)

(11) All the quotations from Brother Felix Fabri are taken from *The Book of the Wanderings of Brother Felix Fabri*, translated by A. Stewart (London Palestine Pilgrims' Text Society, 1887–97)

(12) R. Glaber, *Chronicle*, quoted in *Catholic Encyclopedia* (New York, 1907–14), article on 'Pilgrimage'

(13) All the quotations from the *Guide du Pèlerin* have been translated by the author of the present work from the text established by Mlle Jeanne Vielliard, which is a collation of the Ripoll and Compostela manuscrips (Mâcon, 1963)

(14) I am grateful for most of this information to G. B. Parks *The English Traveler to Italy*, I (Rome, 1954)

(15) The text of this manuscript was edited by C. Horstmann in *Englische Studien*, VIII (1888) and is quoted in modernised form in G. B. Parks *op. cit.*

(16) *Ibid.*

(17) Lambertus Hersfeldensis, *Annales*, in J. P. Migne, *Patrologia Latina* and quoted by G. B. Parks, *op. cit.*

(18) W. Stubbs, *Seventeen Lecturers* (Oxford, 1886)

(19) *Cronica Jocelini*, translated by E. Clarke (London, 1903)

(20) P. Idley, *Instruction to his Son*, edited by C. D'Evelyn (Boston, 1935)

(21) Quoted in G. G. King, *The Way of Saint James*, I (New York and London, 1920) and translated by A. Kendall

(22) I am grateful to G. B. Parks, *op. cit.*, for this information

(23) Quoted in R. Oursel, *Les Pèlerins du Moyen Age* (Paris, 1963) and translated by the author of the present work

(24) E. V. Utterson, *Early Popular Poetry*, I (London, 1817)

(25) Words of the fifteenth-century carol, *Adam lay ybounden*

(26) J. Fox, *Acts of the Martyrs* (London, 1596)

(27) H. F. M. Prescott, *Once to Sinai* (London, 1957)

(28) *De Invectionibus* v. 12, quoted in G. B. Parks, *op. cit.*

(29) E. V. Utterson, *op. cit.*

(30) Ven. Bede, *History of the English Church and People*, translated by L. Shirley-Price (Harmondsworth, 1955)

(31) Bede, *op. cit.*

(32) Adam of Usk, *Chronicon Adae*, edited by E. M. Thompson 2nd ed. (London, 1904)

(33) *Itinerarium cuiusdam anglici* (1344–5) MS Corpus Christi College Cambridge, 370, translated by G. B. Parks

(34) *Indulgentiae ecclesiarum principalium alme urbis Rome* (1474) Huntingdon Library, San Marino, California, G. B. Parks

(35) William Wey, *Itineraries* (Roxburgh Club, 1873) G. B. Parks

(36) Quoted in G. R. Stirling-Taylor, *Canterbury* (London, 1912)

(37) G. R. Stirling-Taylor, *op. cit.*

(38) S. Heath, *In the Steps of the Pilgrims* (London, 1950)

(39) *Ibid.*

(40) *Ibid.*

(41) S. Runciman *op. cit.*, III, 2

(42) T. S. Eliot, *Murder in the Cathedral* (London, 1935)

Index